PENGUIN

MORE THAN

Dave Ramsey knows what it's like to have—and lose—it all. By the age of twenty-six, he had accumulated a real estate portfolio worth more than four million dollars; by the age of thirty, he was so far into debt he was forced to declare personal bankruptcy. Dave Ramsey knows what it's like to lose everything and get it all back. As he was recovering from his real estate losses, Ramsey began teaching others the lessons he had learned the hard way. He has spent the last decade counseling hundreds of thousands of people about personal finance in his seminars and through his thirteen-week course, Financial Peace University, which is taught in thousands of locations nationwide and helping families get out of debt and in control of their money. He is the host of the nationally syndicated radio show, *The Dave Ramsey Show,* which is heard by more than a million people every weekday. The author of the bestselling *Financial Peace, More than Enough,* and *The Financial Peace Planner,* he has been featured on *CBS This Morning, People* magazine, *The Today Show, The Sally Jesse Raphael Show,* and *The 700 Club.* He resides in Nashville, Tennessee, with his wife Sharon and three children, Denise, Rachel, and Daniel.

More Than
ENOUGH

The Ten Keys to Changing Your Financial Destiny

Dave Ramsey

With Thoughts by Sharon Ramsey

PENGUIN BOOKS

PENGUIN BOOKS
Published by the Penguin Group
Penguin Group (USA) Inc., 375 Hudson Street, New York, New York 10014, U.S.A.
Penguin Group (Canada), 90 Eglinton Avenue East, Suite 700, Toronto, Ontario,
Canada M4P 2Y3 (a division of Pearson Penguin Canada Inc.)
Penguin Books Ltd, 80 Strand, London WC2R 0RL, England
Penguin Ireland, 25 St Stephen's Green, Dublin 2, Ireland (a division of Penguin Books Ltd)
Penguin Group (Australia), 250 Camberwell Road, Camberwell, Victoria 3124,
Australia (a division of Pearson Australia Group Pty Ltd)
Penguin Books India Pvt Ltd, 11 Community Centre, Panchsheel Park,
New Delhi – 110 017, India
Penguin Group (NZ), 67 Apollo Drive, Rosedale, North Shore 0632, New Zealand
(a division of Pearson New Zealand Ltd)
Penguin Books (South Africa) (Pty) Ltd, 24 Sturdee Avenue, Rosebank,
Johannesburg 2196, South Africa

Penguin Books Ltd, Registered Offices: 80 Strand, London WC2R 0RL, England

First published in the United States of America by Viking Penguin,
a member of Penguin Putnam Inc. 1999
Published in Penguin Books 2002

60 59 58 57 56 55 54 53 52

Grateful acknowledgment is made for permission to reprint a selection from *A Strategy
for Winning* by Carl Mays. Used by permission of Lincoln Bradley Publishing Group.

PUBLISHER'S NOTE
This publication is designed to provide accurate and authoritative information
in regard to the subject matter covered. It is sold with the understanding that the
publisher is not engaged in rendering financial, accounting or other professional
service. If financial advice or other expert assistance is required, the service
of a competent professional person should be sought.

THE LIBRARY OF CONGRESS HAS CATALOGED
THE HARDCOVER EDITION AS FOLLOWS:
Ramsey, Dave.
More than enough : proven keys to strengthening your family and building
financial peace / Dave Ramsey; with thoughts by Sharon Ramsey.
p.   cm.
ISBN 0-670-88253-4 (hc.)
ISBN 978-0-14-200047-2 (pbk.)
1. Finance, Personal.   2. Finance, Personal—Religious aspects—Christianity.
I. Ramsey, Sharon.   II. Title
HG179.R3155   1999
332.024—dc21   98-31590

Printed in the United States of America
Set in New Caledonia

To my life partner in the quest for **More Than Enough** in relationships and wealth. Without Sharon I would truly be less than half.

To my wonderful and bright children: Daniel, my "mighty man of God"; Rachel, with her zest for life; and Denise, with her sweet spirit.

I love you all with all my heart.

My family is what gives my life meaning, and how we have truly lived lives of **More Than Enough**.

ACKNOWLEDGMENTS

There are so many people who must be thanked on a project this size and without whose help this book would simply not have been possible.

First, to very close and dear friends who helped immensely with input, which you will see throughout these pages:

Pastor L. H. Hardwick   My pastor and spiritual mentor
Dan and Joann Miller   Career coaches
Margaret Phillips   Spirit-filled marriage counselor
Edsel Charles   Bible teacher extraordinaire
Norm and Mary Bess Rollins Attorney and counselor

Sharee Katina, my personal assistant, who served as a reader and first-blush editor.

Joy Strine, who also read as well as helped with editing and writing ideas.

Ken Abraham, who has helped with all our projects and who gave fabulous ideas on this one.

Jane von Mehren, my editor and friend at Viking who believed when we didn't that this book had to happen. Without Jane's confidence and countless hours of effort this project would never have reached critical mass.

CONTENTS

Money is worth nothing to the man
who has more than enough.

—George Bernard Shaw

More Than
ENOUGH

1

More Than Enough What?

Marge's shoulders pitch forward and back, the sobs coming in great waves of grief. As she sobs, the rest of us in the group look nervously around, not sure what to do. When someone is hurting, we want to fix it, but sometimes we know we can't; so we do nothing. Yet Marge's is the kind of grief that is happy in a strange sort of way. Hers is a cleansing cry, the kind of sobbing we make when we are so sorrowful for the mistakes of the past, when we are so happy to be forgiven and so glad to be moving forward with newfound knowledge. It is the groaning sound that comes from a soul being cleansed of the personal flaws that have been destroying our lives or at least holding us back from being who we know we can be. Marge is at the point of rebirth; her life is being born anew from a tattered past cluttered with stupid mistakes, childish mistakes, and peace-robbing mistakes.

All this may seem a little melodramatic for a small group discussion on, of all things, money. Money?! Yes, I dare say one of the best classes in the school of life is money. If we look at our money and how we handle it we learn so much about where we've been, where we are, where we are going, and how we'll get there. Money is a mirror that, strange as it sounds, reflects our personal weaknesses and strengths with amazing clarity. Jesus said it perfectly, "For where your treasure is, there your heart is also." How we handle or mishandle money says volumes about us as people. As we learn new and better behaviors that come from new and better character traits we prosper in money and in soul, and we can find peace.

Marge's story is one I've heard hundreds of times. She and her husband, Jim, were literally passing our Financial Peace office on the way to the divorce attorney to file for divorce. Three different marriage counselors had not been able to get them back together. Marge and Jim were two busy professionals caught up in their careers and the gathering of stuff. They had drifted apart over the eight years of their marriage, way too far apart, and both were now guilty of having affairs. Their trust, respect, and love of each other were now gone—or so they thought. All they felt was pain, raw blinding pain, the kind that makes you cough hard as you cry as if that physical reaction will somehow clean out the pain. Humpty Dumpty is hard to reassemble once broken.

Most marriage counselors do a great job, but marriage counseling had not worked for Marge and Jim. They had swallowed all the pain and anger they could hold. The weird thing was they seemed to have it all: two beautiful children, the teal green Ford Explorer, the fashionable ski boat, and the four-bedroom home in the "right" part of town—you know, the house with the Jacuzzi and the skylight. So with everything working, what went wrong? Why do marriages drift apart? Why do we counsel hundreds of folks—single, married, young, old, tall, short, with children and without, broke, or prosperous—who have reached a point of crisis? Whether the crisis is real, like financial problems, or whether the crisis has evolved from being sick and tired of being a gerbil in a wheel, the people my staff and I talk to are looking at where they are financially and saying, "The price I am paying for these dollars is just too high." People everywhere are saying, *"Enough!* I have got to do something different!" As a society, we are waking up and saying stuff—that new car in the driveway, that Cuisinart in the kitchen, those new suits hanging in the closet, those $100 dinners at fine restaurants—is not enough and we want more. This group of people is seeking out the pain of change because the pain of *same* has gotten too high.

I have been blessed to sit in groups like Marge's thousands of times to watch as people reached a point of such desperation that the pain of keeping on with the same old thing was greater than the pain of change. When the pain of *same* hurts so bad that we consider adjusting our pet behavior, the pain of change is just around the corner.

Not too long ago I too had to learn to change as my wife, Sharon, and I attended that same school of hard knocks when we lost everything we had. After learning the hard way, I have made it my life's mission to help others recover from financial problems and learn to make their own financial opportunities. Having had a front-row seat in the classroom called money that God had chosen to teach us with, I have realized that the lessons money teaches us are not only financial, they are spiritual; they create new character qualities; and they will improve your relationships with your spouse, family, and loved ones. After more than five thousand hours of answering financial questions on "The Money Game," a daily nationally syndicated talk radio show, which claims to be only about money, I have seen again and again that money is just the method that the Great Teacher has chosen to expose and correct our flaws as well as give us "attaboys" for a job well done. In our Financial Peace seminars, I have heard how our financial lessons are really life lessons from over 150,000 folks who wanted more. They don't just want more money, but more from this life, more for their family, more for their community, and more peace.

So Marge's cleansing cry was about a turning point: that event, day, even hour that we can all point back to when our character turns for the better like a heavy oak door on a well-oiled hinge. Those hinge turning times are when we work through the hurt to see clearly the personal changes we must make to be better and avoid the pain of stupid choices. These are valley times as we walk in the valley looking for an opening to get out. The messed-up value system that calls for more work and more stuff at the expense of relationships and peace had brought Marge and Jim to the edge of that cliff we call disaster. Just before they jumped they turned back for one last longing look for what should have been, and while in our group they saw other couples who had healed their value systems, their visions, their hopes, and their marriages. Marge's cleansing cry on this night was the cleansing cry of someone letting go of the guilt and shame of stupid choices. After that night Marge and Jim quickly began to turn their finances and their marriage around. They are now in successful marriage counseling and are well on their way to **MORE THAN ENOUGH**.

I am convinced with everything that is within me that as you apply the concepts in the following chapters to your life, your relationships, and your money, you will begin the process of having **MORE THAN ENOUGH**: more than enough peace and rewards in your relationships, more than enough unity in your marriage, more than enough courage to face the day as a single, more than enough patience to teach your kids the right path, and as time goes on more than enough money. Yes, this is a book about building wealth, but also much more. This is about changing your life, changing your family tree by impacting your children, even changing your community, church, or your entire city. The principles we will explain here are rooted in common sense and reality. These ideas are a proven, time-honored method of implementing values like hard work and diligence, intensity and focus, and patience and contentment, which affect everything that you do. Once you make them a part of your character, everything else, including money and relationships, flows out of them and demands of your life MORE THAN ENOUGH.

As you will see these principles are a strange mix of grandma's common sense, philosophy, theology, and hands-on application. The material in this book has changed my life and thousands of others. It will start you on a journey that is life changing; it is my gift to you, so *use* it. It is useless to learn and not apply the knowledge. Lewis Dunnington said, "You will never leave where you are, until you decide where you'd rather be." I am going to share with you proven principles, which will cause you to build wealth and take your relationships to new heights, but you have to do it. So decide now. Are you ready to face the pain of change so you too can have MORE THAN ENOUGH?

We are about to build a home. This is no ordinary home, this is a mansion with many rooms. This is the MORE THAN ENOUGH Mansion. The MORE THAN ENOUGH Mansion is built carefully and has treasures in every major room. As with any mansion there are many, many rooms and they are all locked. I have the keys. I want to give you the keys to each of the rooms in your life, your character, and your approach to challenges. With these keys you will be able to open the padlocked rooms and discover the treasures that wait for you inside. These are treasures only found in the MORE THAN ENOUGH Mansion and I invite you to add each key to your ring as we go from chapter to chapter.

Keys to the More Than Enough Mansion

1. Change is very hard and we change only when the pain of *same* is greater than the pain of change.
2. Cleansing cries and hinge pins are signals that we are ready.

2

The Missing Link

During the last decade we have taken some good concepts, twisted them, overused them, and finally sickened each other to no end with their constant repeating. Ideas like "paradigm shift" were good to hear the first five hundred times. How about "take it to another level"? Great idea, but if I hear it again I think I'll scream. Another of these overworked terms is "values," or "family values," talk about beat to death. Values started out to mean virtues like truth, loyalty, fairness, compassion—that deep sense of morality where we know what right and wrong are and have the courage to stand up for it. But by the time the politicians and the media got through with using the term for their own purposes, family values had become a relative term. Well, after years of watching people mess up, creating family and financial havoc, I am thoroughly convinced that it is *not* a relative term that can be redefined at your whim to make whatever screw-up you are involved in OK.

Values matter because having principles you live by

brings you joy, peace, and yes, even wealth. Being blown by whatever wind that comes because your personal rudder isn't deep enough or, worse yet, doesn't even exist is to lead a life of fear, confusion, and even destruction. Sadly, family problems and even financial problems are seldom the real problem, but often the symptom of a weak or nonexistent value system. Harsh? Well maybe, but I can speak of these things honestly because I have messed up in my life and have observed thousands of others who brought pain into their lives by straying from a good value system.

MAXING OUT WITH MAX

Take the case of the fifty-two-year-old named Max who called my show one afternoon with a wild story. He told me he had over $128,000 in his 401(k) retirement plan and I congratulated him on saving money so well. He said, "Don't give congratulations too fast because I just spent $23,000 learning a system." After counseling thousands of families in financial crisis I knew what he meant by a "system"; but I knew our audience didn't so I played along. "What kind of 'system' did you spend $23,000 on?" He answered, "Blackjack." He had spent a small fortune on trying to beat Las Vegas at its game. "Did the system work?" I asked, and he said, "If it had worked I wouldn't be calling you, I lost $67,000 in three trips to Vegas." Greed and the get-rich-quick mentality had led him deep into a gambling addiction that cost him his nest egg. By the time penalties and taxes were paid on the retirement account there was just barely enough to cover the $90,000 in credit card debt that his gambling problem had created. Max lost thirty-five years of work and savings in three weekends. Yes, there is a truth you can count on. There is a "good" value system and a bad one, and until you believe that and adjust your behavior to fit, you, like Max, will keep missing out on the best life has to offer.

WISDOM COMES FROM EXPERIENCE

If you have messed up you get another chance starting right now because I'm giving you a "get out of jail free" card. The truth is many of us need second chances. The story of Uncle Zed, an old mountaineer from West Virginia who was celebrated for his wisdom, tells it best:

"Uncle Zed, how did you get so wise?" asked his young nephew.

"Weren't hard," said the old man. "I've got good judgment. Good judgment comes from experience. And experience, well that comes from having bad judgment."

Take your "get out of jail free" card and start implementing the following values in your life and you'll become a man like Uncle Zed.

IT SEEMS SO OBVIOUS

I had a professor in college who, after a lengthy presentation on my part, lowered his glasses down on his nose and said, "Mr. Ramsey you have a firm grasp on the obvious." I feel that way about this first value: integrity. My dictionary defines integrity as the steadfast adherence to truthfulness. The reason many people have trouble prospering is a simple lack of integrity, a lack of truthfulness. Strong statement—so strong you just decided I wasn't talking about you. But think about it for a minute: We all have told lies; we all have struggled with whether to take the heat that being completely honest will eventually bring. Being honest means being honest at tax time, honest with family, honest as in not stealing, and honest with something as simple as following through on appointments and promises. The Bible says, ". . . the little foxes, that spoil the vines." The small violations against our government, our family, our employer, and our relationships begin a pattern of dishonesty.

I am not saying that you must be perfect; none of us are. But if you are in business, when you mess up you must make it better than right. If you are honest, work hard, and provide a good product on time and at a reasonable price, you are guaranteed some level of success. Dr. Thomas J. Stanley, in his research on millionaires, observed this same connection between character and financial success. In his book, *The Millionaire Next Door,* he says, "After twenty years of studying millionaires across a wide spectrum of industries, we have concluded that *the character of the business owner is more important in predicting his level of wealth than the classification of his business.*" What he is saying is that business is like tennis: Those who serve well win. That is integrity.

You have to watch the little things. If you work for someone else and you goof off, you are stealing; that is a lack of honesty. If you take a sick day and you aren't sick, that is stealing. If you say bad things about your manager to someone other than your manager, you are stealing, because you are stealing his ability to lead, cutting productivity, and worst of all you have become just another boring gossip.

INTEGRITY IS NOT JUST FOR THE BUSINESS DAY

You cannot build relationships where there is deception. I recently counseled a young couple in their early twenties who had been married less than two years. She was a very intelligent, beautiful blonde, and he was very athletic and also good looking. You remember seeing this couple in high school, Mr. Football and Ms. Cheerleader. Well, there was trouble in paradise. The young marriage was hanging by a thread because of one simple thing: He spent money and then would lie because he didn't want to face her wrath. His father had always hidden spending from his mom who handled the budget, so that is how he thought marriage worked. And besides, it was harmless wasn't it? He was so immature that he felt, "I work hard and I deserve to spend my money any way I want," and since she had some reasonable, grown-up goals his childish spending angered her.

After trying and failing to convince him that deception was not the foundation of a good relationship, I decided to use my gift of bluntness. At our next counseling session I opened by telling him that we had some very bad news to share with him. I said, "Mr. Football, for the last year Ms. Cheerleader has been having an affair." He first turned red, then green as he became ill, then he became pasty white. Ms. Cheerleader and I let this sink in long enough to have the desired emotional impact and then we told him the truth, which is that she had not had an affair. "You see, Mr. Football, when you lie to Ms. Cheerleader about spending you are breeding the exact same emotions of betrayal, hurt, and mistrust that you just felt. Your spouse takes lying seriously because if you will lie about Home Depot what else will you lie about?" He got the point. Later, as they worked through their budget together, she included reasonable allocations for his shopping sprees. Until trust and respect could be established there was no relationship.

Recently, a woman called in on my radio show and asked how she could invest $20,000 without her husband knowing about it. I told her she didn't need investment advice, she needed a marriage counselor, and she should tell her husband immediately. Of course, she said, "I can't tell him about the money, he'll spend it." But being honest about money is as important as being honest about any other issue.

DECEPTION EQUALS DESTRUCTION

Your marriage and your relationships can only be destroyed by deception. The dating process leading up to marriage is a series of disclosures about everything. Ladies especially want to know everything and you can only err by waiting. There is very seldom a "too soon," but coming clean too late can be perceived as lying. Bob, a single man who had been dating Linda seriously for quite some time almost waited too long to reveal the truth of his own situation because of his shame about his bad finances. I finally convinced him that the bad finances were a minor offense to Linda, but the deception was major. The longer the lie goes on the more disastrous to the relationship the deception becomes. There can be no money secrets from someone you are serious enough about to marry. Do not marry someone without all accounts being laid bare for both of you to see and know what you're getting into; nondisclosure is lying. So if you love someone tell them today where you stand; don't wait. The appointment must be set tonight with your spouse and tell all. Sit down and disclose *all* financial information. Then disclose any personal information your spouse should know about you. If you need a list you missed the point. The point is: NO, NO, NO Secrets!!

SCUMDOG JERKS

You cannot have healthy relationships and build wealth with lies as your foundation. Why do I have to describe this? Because we live in a society today that does not understand the basic actions that integrity requires. A crazy example of how far our culture has dropped in our understanding of integrity around money and relationships is credit card fraud: Some crook, scumdog jerk uses your Social Security number and name to apply for multiple credit cards and then runs up the bill as if there are no consequences. He or she, of course, uses a different address, otherwise you would catch on. This happens to thousands of Americans every year with virtually no way to prevent it, the cost is huge in hassle and fear to the victim, and of course the credit card company has to eat the balance. The weird thing is that the criminal victimizing you is usually a relative, such as a grown child, a parent, or a son- or daughter-in-law. If you use someone else's identity, name, or social security number to obtain credit under false pretenses that is criminal fraud and you are criminal. Because the victim is a bank and/or a relative the criminal usually doesn't feel like they hurt anyone so it must not be wrong. In case I have not been clear, if you are signing someone else's name without a power of attorney you are a criminal and you deserve to go to jail.

Integrity matters. Not only because of the ways it affects other people, but also because of the spiritual and emotional damage that will occur in your life if you don't hold yourself to a very high standard. If you don't hold yourself to an ultrahigh standard it causes you to walk with a limp through life. Take your "get out of jail free" card and correct your course. Integrity matters.

MAN OVERBOARD

Do you feel like I am going overboard? I'm not if you want excellence in your life, relationships, and finances. You see, if you want uncommon results you have to think and do things that are uncommon. If you want things you have never had, you have to do things you have never done. Vince Lombardi said, "The quality of a person's life is in direct proportion to their commitment to excellence, regardless of their chosen field of endeavor." If you want to have more joy and more wealth than most people do you have to live more excellently than they do. Living excellently doesn't mean simply being efficient, it means living with superhigh integrity, with loyalty, and with commitment to a value system as a solid foundation. So maybe it is time to go "overboard."

What does it mean to go overboard? It means that you are someone like Willis Reed. Remember the 1973 NBA finals? Reed had injured his leg and was unable to play, but when the championship was on the line he hobbled out onto the court and played several crucial minutes, giving his Knicks teammates the emotional boost they needed to go all the way. Reed was the captain of the team and by entering the game at that moment, he showed his teammates, the fans, and his opponents that he was a man with character, integrity, and passion. That's going overboard!

I have used this same principle in my own business. God has blessed me with some wonderful people to work with as our company has grown. The huge growth rate we have experienced and the dynamic nature of it has meant that entire jobs have been done away with. We then formed bigger and better opportunities for our team members, and in that state of flux there have been a lot of pay plans that have had to be reworked. I have been blessed to watch the loyalty and commitment that a team's members will bring you when you treat them right. More important, I have learned why people succeed and fail based on how their personal integrity causes them to deal with change. Some will pout, cry, moan, and decide to get back at the boss; they reap heartache and job loss. Others will take a pay cut to get in on the crusade and concentrate on the horizon; they reap joy, fulfillment, bonuses, and promotions. If this joy, fulfillment, and increased pay doesn't happen on my team someone will steal my team members and give them what they deserve. Over the long term you get what you deserve, and none of us like it when what we deserve is pain.

RESPONSIBILITY HAS TO BE PERSONAL

I am not a licensed or degreed psychologist, but I believe that traditional Freudian views of psychotherapy have done more to harm our nation's values than any philosophy to come along in years. The concept of digging in the graveyard of your past to find what caused your faults has some merit when used to identify wounds and heal them, but too often we are taught to blame our lot in life on others. It was our mean, nasty old parents; it was that we weren't the firstborn; it was our brother who tortured us; it was our sister who got all the attention. Bull! Thousands and thousands of people who had horrible childhoods thrive and even prosper in relationships and wealth. Why do they prosper? Because they made a decision that their fate is up to them, that it is their own personal responsibility.

Albert Schweitzer said it well: "Man must cease attributing his problems to his environment, and learn again to exercise his will, his personal responsibility." Enough whining, I am sick of whining, whining by every special interest group, whining against our upbringing, whining against the mean old boss, whining against your pastor, whining about your spouse—especially if it's an ex-spouse—just whining. Whining is a sign of a lack of character on your part. If you don't like the way something is, *do* something about it. Finger-pointing, blame shifting, and whining, while they appear to have merit, are not doing something. There is tremendous energy in positive activity and in providing a solution. That activity, while it may not solve the problem, moves you from being self-centered to solution-centered.

IT MATTERS TO THIS ONE

For years, motivational speakers have told the starfish story and it makes the point, so here goes: A storm had caused thousands of starfish to be washed ashore on the beach. As the early morning sun was coming up it became apparent that thousands of them would die that morning. A man walking down the beach looking at this sad sight noticed a boy throwing a starfish back into the ocean. The man in his fatherly wisdom walked up to the boy, placed his hand on his shoulder, and said, "Son, you can't save all these starfish, they are going to die. What does it matter?"

"It matters to this one," the boy replied and threw another in.

Do something to impact your situation, take responsibility, because you aren't anyone else's job. Yes, we all get kicked, get a bad break, had horrible things happen to us. It takes a little while to recover your strength when you get punched, but after the appropriate grieving and healing we must make the decision to make lemonade from lemons. When bad stuff happens resist the human urge to blame and instead join the elite group called the doers.

GETTING OUT OF THE TIGER CAGE

Clifford G. Baird, in his tape series on change, tells a tremendous story about the power of personal responsibility. He had just met a man whom he called his hero. This man was a fighter pilot in Vietnam and after flying several missions was shot down and taken captive by the enemy. His captors used a bamboo tiger cage to imprison him. The cage was not tall or long enough for him to be able to stretch out at any time. This prisoner was made to walk daily carrying the cage with his feet through the bottom bars as the patrol went from place to place. The captors took him with them in case they met with the other side and needed to trade him for one of their comrades being held prisoner. This man spent four and a half years in this cage. When asked how he maintained his sanity for all those years and how he finally escaped, he said that he remembered from his high school psychology class about REM sleep being deep sleep. So each night when his captors would go to sleep he would count to four thousand. By waiting for their deep sleep he was then safe to check the bars, every single bar on the cage, every single night for four and a half years. Can you imagine the night that finally a bar moved? Can you imagine how much focus it must have taken in that moment of excitement to have the patience to pack mud around the bar so the breaking sound would not be heard? He broke free and stumbled through the jungle, hiding for another week, until he found American troops and aid. The doctors examining him said he would have died from the harsh captivity in just another ninety days. That man took responsibility for his circumstances, knowing that no one else was coming and that he better find a way to live.

Those who live life large know that Rambo is not coming and neither is Ed McMahon. You better rise up, leave the cave, kill something, and drag it home. Sometimes people who are hurting will challenge me on this concept, saying that prosperity and a great family life are only for those few hearty souls that God seems to bless from the womb. Not true! I have been blessed to see ordinary people—extremely ordinary people from all walks of life, many with crippling situations—make a decision to take control. Take the case of Julia Tavalaro who thirty years ago had a stroke that left her dead to the world. Her husband left her, the nursing staff at the home she was in ignored her, everyone assumed she was a vegetable. In fact, she was and is very much alive inside, and after more than twenty years of trying to somehow convey that her brain was functioning completely normally, she finally managed, with the help of two therapists, to communicate. Working with a writer, she wrote her remarkable story in a powerful memoir called *Look Up for Yes*.

Wrest control from life, take control from circumstances by simply realizing that it is worth the trouble to become the person you know God made you to be. St. Ambrose said it like this: "Work like it all depends on you and pray like it all depends on God." Taking responsibility not only for our mistakes so that we don't repeat them, but taking responsibility for making whatever change is necessary to get where we should go is of vital value in the person who prospers.

CONNECTION IS KEY

People who have More Than Enough also value strong connected relationships with those they love. I am not talking about merely living in the same house, living on the same street, working with or going to church with people. Two gerbils in a wheel passing each other and nodding are not a strong connected relationship. It is not asking how someone is doing and hoping they won't really tell you. A connected relationship requires an investment that few folks make anymore. Gary Smalley, a Christian marriage writer, says when it comes to the people we love, love is spelled *T-I-M-E*.

WE NEED SIDEWALKS

A workaholic gerbil in a wheel invented the stupid phrase "quality time." There is no question that quantity time is what is needed to develop strong fruitful relationships. We are failing miserably in this culture by not slowing down enough to enjoy each other. Dan Scott, a pastor in Tennessee, preached a wonderful sermon once in which he made the point that we no longer build sidewalks between homes because we no longer visit our neighbors. We do however build jogging paths, which is what a gerbil in a wheel needs since he's always running, never getting anywhere.

When I was growing up in the sixties, my mom would often be found at a neighbor's kitchen table having a cup of coffee at midmorning while the kids played. These women were there for each other, the older and wiser giving good advice, the breaking marriages supported, the kids cared for, whatever it took. The evenings would find half the neighborhood gathered on a deck or patio to enjoy a night of interaction. We camped together, the men fished together, and as a kid you could get your butt busted by any adult in the neighborhood. There was a real sense of community. We didn't have babies shooting babies in the schoolyard.

What has stolen our ability to find those luxurious hours to invest in family and friends? Several things have stolen that time. We are so marketed to that we have started to believe that more stuff will make us happy. But in this country, more stuff has resulted in more debt. What debt means is that we end up spending our every waking hour working to pay off our bills. And while today there are many more opportunities for women to work out of the home, statistics show that this second income is being used in large part simply to try to keep up with the Joneses and ahead of the bill collector. *USA Today* reported several amazing differences in the 1960s family and the 1990s family using many government agencies as their source. The typical house in 1960 was 1,375 square feet, 1 story, with 3 bedrooms and 1.5 baths while the typical house in the 1990s is 1,940 square feet, 2 stories, 4 bedrooms, and 2.5 baths. The median new home price in the 1960s was $20,000 compared with the 1990s median home price of $133,900. What we used to consider a small mansion is now a starter home, and we stamp our feet like a spoiled child, yelling, "I won't settle for anything less because I deserve it." In the sixties, 37 percent of women worked in the workplace as opposed to 57 percent today. The result has been that while household incomes, after adjustment for inflation, have risen from $25,866 in the 1960s to $38,782 in the 1990s, necessities like food, transportation, utilities, and shelter have dropped as a percentage of income. I am not saying it is wrong for a woman to be in the workplace, but I am saying that the research shows she doesn't have to be in the workplace since her income has gone to more stuff and is not needed for survival. While some ladies have decided to leave home for a career, an amazing number of the women we communicate with want to be at home with the kids. The problem is they can't because of the payments on the stuff that, oddly enough, was going to make them happy. Seems almost as if the very thing we thought would make us happy (stuff) has stolen the thing that among others brings us the most happiness: relationships, real connected time-invested relationships. Relationships with our spouses, our kids, our friends, and our coworkers are the real stuff of a MORE THAN ENOUGH life.

MARKETING ROBS PEACE

Marketing has entered our homes and has stolen our peace. I may be weird, but when I consider that we have chosen to watch *Seinfeld* instead of cooking dinner for a sick neighbor something is very wrong. Realize that entertainment venues have caused our nation to lose its relationship soul. Yes, I am saying television, the Internet, and Nintendo, while entertaining, have stolen those after-work hours when families, neighbors, and congregation members used to do things for each other as well as play together. How long has it been since you played board games, card games, tossed a ball, or just had a cup of coffee with a hurting friend? These wonderful electronic gadgets with 120 channels or thirty-two levels of Tomb Raider or Doom are stealing our quantity time. They are not evil and you can tell by my familiarity that they are in our home; but we are not afraid to turn them off—nor should you be.

DRIFTING IS SUBTLE

John and Marsha, a couple we met when they came through our thirteen-week personal finance boot camp, reflect many people today. John was a pharmaceutical salesman and Marsha a mid-level manager. Together they were making "good money," over $75,000 per year, and after twelve years of marriage they came to us to learn to make their money work harder. They were two powerful, intelligent, and independent people who each had their own finances—separate checkbooks, separate 401(k)s, separate mutual funds. Part of our program, as I will explain later, forces couples to combine finances, checkbooks, savings, and budgets. The communication involved in that process forced John and Marsha to realize that they never talked anymore, that they had grown apart, way apart. The class was very hard on them because they had to admit they had lost that strong connection—I think they call it love. They had "evolved" through years of pursuing their careers and stuff into two moneymaking robots living under the same roof. They were too tired at night to really enjoy time together, too stressed to do anything except unwind in front of the mind-numbing TV, go to sleep, get up the next day and get back in the wheel like all good little gerbils.

What these sophisticated professionals learned is one of the cardinal lessons of the MORE THAN ENOUGH life: If the two of you aren't in harmony with your money, you aren't really in harmony at all. They had come in to learn investments and instead they saved a marriage, a marriage that they didn't even realize was in trouble. Marsha and John reevaluated their value system and decided like so many others have that time together was more important than a stupid $25,000 car, or a lake house, or a . . . well, you get the picture. They scaled their lifestyle down, got out of debt, and now a mere three years later have more money, more time, and definitely a better marriage. I saw John

and Marsha just the other day and they were like twenty-
year-old newlyweds; they couldn't keep their hands off
each other!

WHEN SHE EARNS MORE

In more and more households the wife is not only a major
part of the bread winning, she is outearning her husband.
Ladies in Fortune 500 company boardrooms used to be
nonexistent, and now it is hard to find a successful company or industry without high-earning and capable ladies
in the driver's seat. That is great in the workplace, but
even in these enlightened days, when that lady gets home
with the higher income it brings special challenges to the
marriage. Right or wrong these challenges exist and are
very real. I remember Doris, a very successful attorney
making over $200,000 a year, pleading with me in a coun-
seling session to provide some solution to the stress her income brought to her husband. Pete was successful in his
own right as a sales rep making almost $70,000 per year,
nothing to sneeze at. I remember looking at the pain in
Doris's eyes as she described Pete's constant bent toward
wild-eyed, get-rich-quick schemes that we all knew were
driven by his need to catch up. She told of the thousands
of dollars lost in his bad deals that she had agreed to spend
their household income on. The pain in her eyes was not
from the money lost, but instead the same pain a mother
has when she knows her child is looking for significance in

places he can't find it. Pain that comes from thinking that somehow by going through the blood, sweat, and tears of law school, sitting for the bar, and ultimately realizing her goal only to find that this left her husband feeling a need to "catch up."

Doris is not the type that wanted to "rule" the household. On the contrary, she was a little too laid back, not giving her input for fear that would add to her husband's insecurity. Nor was Pete some kind of wimp. They are healthy, intelligent people experiencing natural stress in their marriage, a stress that no other generation has had to face. How did they solve this situation? By realizing that even enlightened, educated men are task-oriented and have egos. No, Doris did not quit and become barefoot and pregnant. But by simply talking about the issue, voicing the fact that almost any man, especially one with ambition, will feel that he is coming up short when his wife earns more, they have been able to overcome most of the relationship stress. Maybe it shouldn't be, but that is simply life. Doris can never play the trump card in a fight that she earns more because that opens deep wounds. Pete can't go on get-rich-quick schemes as a method of catching up. He has to find other ways to express his masculinity. With a marriage counselor tune-up every six months or so and some ground rules that include tons of communication, they have not solved this natural stress point but have learned to manage it, so that they prosper financially and in their relationship.

Connection, strong connection, takes time and lots of

being very real. Around the subject of money, being real is something that is hard for most of us even with our closest loved ones. Most people are more prone to talk about sex than money.

THE SHE-BEAR ON HER OWN

This strong connection to others takes on a whole different kind of intensity with the single mom. Left to raise the cubs alone the she-bear gets bent on sheer survival. Given the circumstances that she finds herself in the single mom is one of the most noble of animals. Whatever the cause of her situation, most single moms find themselves very exposed. Consider the following items:

1. On average, women earn 74 percent of what men do.
2. After a divorce, 90 percent of kids stay with their moms according to the Census Bureau.
3. Not all dads are deadbeats, but a disturbing number pay child support too little, too late, or not at all. The U.S. Department of Health and Human Services says that 27 percent of fathers completely default on child support and many more pay late or partial payments.
4. A study conducted at Princeton University and reported on in an article in the *Atlanta Journal-Constitution* concluded that half of single-parent families in the United States live below the poverty line.
5. When shopping for big-ticket items, such as cars, or ne-

gotiating for major repairs, women are likely to be victimized by overcharging. Remar Sutton in his book on buying cars, *Don't Get Taken Every Time*, says that women are among the favorite targets of salesmen who don't have their best interests at heart.

STATISTICS IMITATING LIFE

I have watched these statistics come to life in my office as I have sat with that single mom trying to make a budget stretch farther than can be done. She is frustrated, beat down, tired, and feels as if there is no hope. Yes, single mom, I am on your side. So what do you do? Your situation is so dire, how can a bunch of values help you, you ask? Values are the tools that you, like the rest of us, use to lay the foundation to win. As I said before, avoid the blame game. Yes, you have plenty to be angry about, but that will not solve your challenges. Your ex-husband may be a jerk, but he is your *ex*-husband, gone, not there, out of the way; it is time to get on with the rest of living. Now that your man is gone, learn about all those things he was expert at; learn more about cars or whatever subjects are necessary to keep you from constantly getting ripped off. If you haven't been able to bone up on your auto mechanics as of yet, ask a neighbor or friend to help you when you negotiate with the mechanic at the garage.

Next, you must decide today that stupid financial decisions that feel good for the moment will destroy your ability to win in the long term. Often this means making decisions that cause present heartache or difficulty, but which will save you money and a whole lot more heartache down the road. Thousands of single moms fall into the same financial pits.

Pit number one: Keeping the house. Most single moms can't afford the family home. Ouch! The kids have been through enough and now I am so unfeeling as to suggest that they now move and leave their friends at school. But unless you have a very unusual financial situation you are trying to keep a home on about 30 percent of your former household income. The math doesn't work and the long-term prosperity of your new situation depends on your shedding this burden. Sadly, most single moms will not hear this advice because their wonderful and powerful she-bear protect-the-kids-at-all-costs instinct is at a twelve on a scale of one to ten. This instinct will typically cause the single mom to keep the home she can't afford until it is lost, until it is too run-down to sell at a great price, or other situations that cause a ten-year financial setback. Home is where your heart is, so get a modest and affordable dwelling. Begin your new life and the new life for the kids from a solid financial footing, not one based on the past. Your children will survive and prosper not based on their friends, not based on the house they live in, but based on your making home wherever they are.

Pit number two: Giving the kids everything they want so that they will feel better. Frederick Morrison, a psychology professor at Loyola University, says, "Plagued by guilt, single parents tend to put even more energy into their children than married ones do." I will second that motion. I have observed some ridiculous purchases made by single parents thinking that the child would "feel better." You can't spend your way out of guilt. They will not feel better except maybe for about ten minutes. All you are doing is medicating their stress with your spending. Even if you can afford it, which you probably can't, you are teaching them some really bad values. Feel bad? Spend. Dumb, really dumb. Why am I being so blunt? It's because I have had she-bears get violent with me for suggesting that purchasing $178 tennis shoes while the electric bill isn't paid is stupid. There is an old Danish proverb that says if you give a child everything he wants when he cries and a pig everything he wants when he grunts you will have a fine pig and a sorry child.

Sacrificing the long-term financial health of you and your kids to cover guilt, fix current pain, or keep disruption down may get you a nobility badge but at the end of the day you will not reach your real goal. We all share the same goal: to raise healthy well-balanced children within our incomes, whatever our income is.

Pit number three: Impulse or fatigue spending. As a single parent, you have to do everything. Get the oil changed, go to the cleaners, pick up the sick child, and cook when you get home. All this makes you physically and emotionally tired. With fatigue can come a pity party that says "I deserve a break today." Many single parents, who can least afford to, do a lot of restaurant impulsing and purchase way too many prepared foods that are much more expensive.

Single parent, I am giving you your own "get out of jail free" card and it's called "asking for help." Slow down, commit to less, and give yourself permission to schedule a family member, neighbor, or church friend to watch the children for free once a week while you relax and make better decisions. To the rest of us: If you know a single parent (ha! we all do), offer to baby-sit, give them a night off. God knows they need it.

Single dads with the responsibility of raising the kids, I am not ignoring you. After thousands of counseling situations, however, I have observed that on average you are faring much better financially than the single mom. But you still must watch out for the same pitfalls. I know you don't have it easy, so take heart, inspiration, and instruction from these pages.

While single parents face special challenges, you can still enjoy the MORE THAN ENOUGH life. Carl Mays writes of a single mom whose efforts made a winner of her son in his book *A Strategy for Winning:*

> In the early 40s a mother of several children was determined to keep her family together when her husband died. She worked at four different jobs: waiting tables, cleaning offices, working in a bakery and delivering coal in Pittsburgh where she lived. Later she took the civil service exam and eventually became the chief bookkeeper for the city treasurer.

She held her family together with love and strength. She couldn't give her children money but she did teach them courage and the meaning of character.

One of her children wanted to play football in college but none of the large colleges to which he applied wanted him. They said he was too little and too slow. So he played for a small college and excelled. Then he wanted to play professional football and tried out for his hometown Pittsburgh Steelers but was cut from the team in short order.

He found a job in construction, helping to build some of the skyscrapers you can see today in Pittsburgh. But he didn't give up on his dream. He chose how to respond to rejection. He didn't see himself as a victim of circumstances, helpless to do anything about it. He didn't curse his size and develop a bias against larger men. Here's what he did: He looked at his options and decided to play in a league that paid him $6 per game where he could improve his skills. He continued to write and telephone NFL teams in hopes of an opportunity to try out. After seven months of asking, he received an invitation to try out for the Baltimore Colts. The rest is sports history. Johnny Unitas, honored in the NFL Hall of Fame, was one of the greatest quarterbacks to ever play the game.

Unitas was the son of a single mom who passed on values, not money. Single moms, you can win. She did!

WHEN TWO FAMILIES BECOME ONE

The family counselor's nightmare, the blended family, has also entered my office for financial counseling, giving me a taste of the challenges these families face. And because how we handle our money represents priorities and the flow of power in the family, the blended family can be very explosive on the issue of money. The "yours," "mine," and "ours" emotions run deep and run high. The parents can be torn deeply if there is any indication of favoritism. The kids are not only sensitive on issues of money, they will use it to drive wedges between parents. They also do that in a family where there has been no divorce and remarriage, and where there are no feelings of guilt, failure, or need to protect turf, but in the blended family the manipulation by kids can become an art form. I have seen teenagers and even grown children with kids of their own with self-centeredness beyond belief. These folks can virtually destroy a second marriage. Those of you in blended families know the volatility that you face and know that with love and principled guidelines even the blended family with all its challenges can work.

Prepare yourselves before the marriage. If you are considering marriage where there are children in the home, get some serious premarital counseling. Sadly many people think they are just marrying the person they've been dating, and of course there is much more to it. Sit down with your spouse-to-be and write down how the parenting and money management will be done. This ensures that the communication is clear. Sounds more like a business merger than a marriage, doesn't it? Actually, it is infinitely more complicated. No, I am not suggesting a prenuptial agreement. I am suggesting that all the parenting rules, including the flow of money, be agreed upon so there are no surprises.

Return to the basics if you are already in a blended family. I know you love your kids. So do I, but mine know their mom comes first. While saying your spouse comes first sounds harsh, research has proven it is the best gift you can give your children's self-esteem. In addition you are modeling a successful marriage for them. If you allow your child from a former marriage to set the terms of your new marriage through money manipulation, you will never have that wonderful marriage you dream of. When children rule any family, we call that dysfunctional. And once you're in the midst of a dysfunctional situation, it's hard to get out of it. But by sitting down with your spouse and agreeing, in writing, on parenting and money management issues, you will be able to work together to improve the entire family's situation.

Once you and your spouse have agreed on how to handle these issues, you should communicate what is appropriate to your children. When there are teenagers in the blended family, we suggest the contract method. With your teenage child, agree to a set of money and household guidelines and write them down. Then when stepdad wants the yard cut it doesn't seem like he is being "unfair."

Tons of love, hugs, and communication are your best

bets in any family, but especially in the blended family. If you are in a blended family watch for symptoms of negative emotions around the subject of money. Money can be the light that exposes wounds or other problems in the midst of a volatile setting. Please remember you can't spend your way out of guilt. You are kidding yourself if you think the child that is hurting is going to be made better by spending.

Before we leave the subject of values and how they affect the MORE THAN ENOUGH relationships and wealth building we must look at passing on these values to the next generation.

TEACH THE CHILDREN

James Baldwin says that children have never been very good at listening to their elders, but they have never failed to imitate them. Your children cannot hope to have MORE THAN ENOUGH without a strong values foundation. Integrity, personal responsibility, character, loyalty, and connectedness in relationships can't be taught; it must be *modeled*. We can look for teachable moments as we raise our children. When they are small we can mold their direction, but as they reach the dreaded teenage years our only shot at finishing the transfer of strong values is the mentor approach. The mentor knows that when a value is violated that creates a teachable moment. That violation opens the door to show not just the short-term consequences of lying, but that the foundation of a long and prosperous life is eroded and that integrity (for example) has far-reaching fingers. As parents, teachers, and leaders of children our future depends on our pouring our lives into them, taking the time to complete the mentoring task of handing over the baton of values. As we go through our journey toward **MORE THAN ENOUGH**, we will share specific lessons and methods for teaching your children the values that matter.

VALUES REALLY DO MATTER

Values affect the inflow and the outflow of money. How you handle or mishandle your money tells us who you are and, more important, it tells *you* who you are. Your priorities, passions, goals, and fears are shown clearly in the flow of your money. Your value system or lack of one causes money to flow around you, past you, or to you. When money is in your possession what you do with it screams loudly who you are. We all want things that last. Stuff doesn't last. Clothes wear out or it takes them twenty-five years to come back into fashion, too long to wait. Cars break down, shoes wear out, your computer is already out of date, your TV is too small, your furniture is worn out, and your boat is too slow. Even the faces on Mount Rushmore are cracking and need constant repair. Stuff just won't do it for you. We all need something that will last.

Observing the alienation that pervades many of the twentieth century's affluent, industrialized societies, the psychologist Victor E. Frankl pondered the plight of those who "have enough to live by, but not enough to live for," who seemed to have "the means, but no meaning." What I have observed is that if you will return to the meaning the means will chase you down and tackle you. Do the things that are important in ways that are noble and you will be led to **MORE THAN ENOUGH**.

Dan Miller, a leading career counselor, says values cause the results because from values flow beliefs, then attitudes, which result in behaviors and actions. Those behaviors and actions determine whether we will have **MORE THAN ENOUGH**. Your values determine how effective you will be at getting **MORE THAN ENOUGH**.

READY FOR A TEST?

Values represent the first of the principles involved in attaining **MORE THAN ENOUGH**. Each principle in this book builds on the next. Before continuing, take this self-test: Spend at least fifteen minutes of very quiet time clearing your mind and thinking about the answers to the following questions:

1. What missing or twisted value has been holding me back?
2. What could I do this week that would give me more connection to my spouse, my child, or my best friend?
3. Are there any ways that I could better show my boss my loyalty to my job and my coworkers?

4. Have I been lying to someone I love because I'm afraid to face their anger?
5. Do I view values and character as something that is old-fashioned or out of date? If so, what is my life missing that those people of another generation had?
6. What activities am I involved in that I could fire myself from that would simplify my life?
7. What can my mate and I do better to model foundational values to our children?
8. Am I taking advantage of teachable moments and mentoring with my teenagers?

We all have a couple of issues and values to work on. And by working on them we can lay that solid foundation that will allow us to achieve MORE THAN ENOUGH. Re-lay it if needed. Lay that foundation for yourself and then pass it on to your children and to others you can have influence over. Without a strong value system you will never have MORE THAN ENOUGH. Values are the missing link.

THE STORY BEGINS

Core *values* lay the foundation of all the other proven keys for MORE THAN ENOUGH. From this point we will build a progressive story, but always remember that all the other keys find their roots in *values.*

Thoughts from Sharon . . .

Over the years the values for "The Ramsey Family" have developed into honesty, respect, love, and forgiveness. The respect value is a particularly important key in raising children.

I am reminded of it often when I have to tell our children when they are arguing with each other, "If you can't say something nice, then don't say anything at all." When they hear this they know they have misused the respect value.

When you learn to respect others, adults and children, you will see yourself improve in self-esteem, happiness, and fulfillment.

As children become adults, the values you as parents instill in them will carry over, and they will pass them on to their children, and so on. The four basic values in our family are ones everyone can benefit from. It all starts at home with your spouse and children and flows out to the world from your nest.

Keys to the More Than Enough Mansion

1. Change is very hard and we change only when the pain of *same* is greater than the pain of change.
2. Cleansing cries and hinge pins are signals that we are ready.
3. Values really do matter and real values are the foundation of everything to come.
4. Integrity—real deep integrity, even with the little things—is vital because deception destroys.
5. Connectedness is key; take time to use the sidewalks that connect you to family, friends, and coworkers.

3

Victory Through Vision

T-G-I-F (Thank God It's Friday) is the battle cry of the weekend party animal and the battle cry of most of working America. We live in a culture in which surveys estimate that as many as 67 percent of workers dislike their jobs, so is it any wonder we have learned to say "Thank God it's Friday" and "Oh God, it's Monday"?

Proverbs 29:18 says, "Where there is no vision, the people perish." Perish as in die? Yes. When we surrender vision, we surrender our dreams, our hopes, and reach a despair or, worse yet, a level of apathy as thick as syrup. Having vision does not mean that all of a sudden your life will become easy, but as we will see, it will guide you toward your dreams and the **MORE THAN ENOUGH** life. It will also help you when life beats you up. After you have suffered a setback or some sort of failure, you can develop the wrong kind of vision: tunnel vision focused on survival. You lose your ability to see. Clifford G. Baird, a motivational speaker, says, "We can end up looking at life through a straw, instead of seeing things the way they are."

Tunnels steal light and limit your thoughts and goals; tunnel vision will ultimately bring you the pain you were trying to avoid. "Thank God It's Friday" doesn't bring MORE THAN ENOUGH; it doesn't even bring enough.

Vision is vital. The values you learned about in the previous chapter laid the foundation, giving you the ability to have vision. Vision that is rooted in values is the only vision that will last. Vision that has no foundation and depth in values is merely a dream, and you will wake up disappointed.

GETTING OUT OF THE FOG

When you are a child, vision is like a dream complete with unclear plots and fog. You think, I want to be an astronaut when I grow up, even though you hate to fly. Or, I really have to have a pony, even though you live in the middle of a large city. Or, I will get an A on my math test, even though you haven't studied. For a child, vision is a kind of magical thinking about things that might happen in the future if only, somehow, everything goes just right. Many adults think about their dreams and visions in just the same way as children do: If I'm lucky, if only somehow everything goes right . . .

When you have walked with those who have real vision, however, you understand it simply means sight, very clear sight. When asked if she knew of anything worse than being blind, Helen Keller once said, "Yes, being able to see and having no vision." The ability to see doesn't mean having 20/20 vision; it means being able have a clear picture of your vision and how you plan to achieve it.

Interestingly, in many sports we are taught to look not at where we are, but where we want to go. Literally, the way in which you position and hold your body determines your athletic success. In high school, I water-skied in competition. When jumping or doing slalom runs we learned quickly that you follow the direction of your head. Head down, fall, and head up, success. You go where you look when skiing and in life. Look down and stay down; look up with vision and sight, then you will move toward fulfillment and **More Than Enough**. You will never have **More Than Enough** until you make having a vision a habit. Choosing to see is a discipline and comes by doing it on purpose.

DOLLARS AND VISION

Why do you need vision? To start with, it affects income. Studies of people who earn $100,000 a year or more and have maintained that income level for years reveal an interesting character trait. These six-figure earners all think in five-year blocks (or more) of time. They are very unconcerned about today except for how today is a building block toward their vision, which may not be fully realized for another twenty years. They think long term in all decisions. Six-figure earners think about the long-term implications of every move they make and don't make those moves unless they move them one step closer to their vision. These are happy people not because they have six figures to spend (although that doesn't hurt) but because temporary pain is just that: It is temporary. If you think long term you become a saver and an investor. As an investor with a long-term mentality (vision) you don't panic when the mutual fund drops, because you are looking at what the market has done over ten years and not what today brings. Saving and investing with vision makes you rich. This is one of the reasons the rich get richer. Bad times are correctly viewed as temporary setbacks and a time to learn. You can walk through the sewage that life sometimes puts in front of you and barely notice because you have your eye on the horizon rather than constantly looking at your current circumstances.

The other side of the coin continues to prove our point. The folks at the bottom end of the income brackets who stay there tend to share the character trait of short-term thinking, making decisions based on short-term results. That sounds harsh doesn't it? Well, if you think short term you rent to own your VCR and get ripped off. You pawn items or fall for these jerk cash advance businesses that cash hot checks, cash advances at 650 percent annual percentage rate in most states. If you think short term you work for the weekend and fall prey to pleasure-based products that in the end steal your pleasure. If you think short term you don't save and invest so you can't build wealth. When you think short term, if you do invest you can't leave the money alone so you end up buying high, selling low, then thinking: "I have the worst luck." Luck had nothing to do with it, you simply shortchanged your-self by not carrying through on your vision. Short-term thinking is why the poor get poorer. Those who realize this are those who don't remain poor. Mike Todd states this matter of the heart well when he says, "I have never been poor, only broke. Being poor is a frame of mind." Those who are given the gift of vision by a parent, a mentor, or God start to think long term and say things like, "I am get-ting my degree no matter what and nothing will stop me." And they *do* it.

TEST TIME

It's time to test your financial vision. Do you have one? If you don't this chapter and test are your wake-up call!

1. What size nest egg will you need to retire with dig-nity if you pull 8 percent annually from the growth? (Hint: Divide the income you want by .08 to get the number.)
2. Now that you have your nest egg amount how much do you need to save per month to get there, with inflation? (Hint: See the form in the back called Retirement Monthly Planning to help you.)
3. How about your kids' college fund? How much do you need and how much do you have to save to get there?
4. When do you estimate you will need a replacement car? How much will it cost you? Do the division to see how

much of a car payment you have to pay *yourself* so you can avoid car debt.

5. When will you need some furniture replaced or other major purchase made? Do the math, figure out how much you need to put aside this month and every month until you can pay cash for it.

6. Are you ready for Christmas? It is in December this year. How much will you spend? Now divide that amount by the number of months left until Christmas and voilà! You have a Christmas savings program for a debt-free Christmas—you know, peace on earth, good-will to men.

7. Vacation paid for? Do the math and pay cash. Debt-free vacations are a whole lot more fun.

8. How much money will it take to permanently change your family tree—$10 million? If you start now you probably can save that much with the power of compound interest.

9. How much money would it take to start a college in your name? Yes, let us get crazy!!!! You see you can do anything if you have a powerful enough vision and the time to play out the details.

10. What is your wildest financial dream? Play with the math to make it into a vision, then it may actually become a goal. Vision is powerful.

ON THE JOB

Confucius says if a man will find work he loves he will never have to work another day in his life. Vision means understanding that a *job* will never satisfy and that taking a position just for the money will never lead to MORE THAN ENOUGH. People who work for money only are usually miserable, because there is no fulfillment and no meaning to what they do. I have some friends who we will rename Rachel and Mark who hold master's degrees and could easily earn more than $100,000 per year, but instead live on less than $10,000 per year as missionaries traveling the world to spread the gospel. They are some of the most fulfilled and happy people I have ever met, always upbeat and with another exciting story to tell. Their marriage is great, they have raised great kids, and they are living a life of MORE THAN ENOUGH. You should find your gift and passion and work in a vocation that utilizes those things. People who live out their vision, their dreams in their career, usually don't make much now, but become the Bill Gateses, Steven Speilbergs, and the Michael Jordans of the world.

Consider that in America today, the average time we stay in a job is an astounding 3.2 years. If you have your sights set merely on a job, that is not vision. You will have constant worry, lack of creativity, and income problems if your vision or sight is limited to one job. The people who have vision are not looking at jobs, but rather at career paths. A career path may take you through several jobs throughout your life.

TURNING VISION INTO WEALTH

We have all been told we should save for retirement, save for that house we want to buy, save for our kids' college education. Why do some of us—no matter our incomes—over and over again fail to do these things we know we should? We lack vision; it is vision that says, "I'd rather have a hen tomorrow than an egg today." Yet we live in a society that tells us to take the egg now, rather than wait for the chicken. It is that same society that is fighting the last round of terminal cancer on social insecurity; we are losing that battle because we have on an individual level and on a governmental level chosen eggs over hens for so long, we are left with only egg on our faces.

IT IS NOT ROCKET SCIENCE

Wealth building is affected by vision. The irony is that investing for retirement and college is not rocket science. Ninety percent of investing is just doing it, not the details of the investment. We recommend types of investments like mutual funds, but which fund or when to get in the market is overrated as investor savvy, while just doing it doesn't get the press it deserves. After years of helping people with setting financial goals that will allow them to realize their vision I have found that the biggest problem is not where or when to invest, but simply the choice between investing and spending on toys. Vision will make you an investor instead of a consumer; it will make you think ahead five, ten, or twenty years instead of only thinking about today or tomorrow.

Making your vision a reality takes time. It takes the time to calculate how your money could be the power behind your vision. Consider this: You are a teenager who puts $2,000 into a Roth IRA on your sixteenth and seventeenth birthdays. If those two Roth IRAs were invested in a growth stock mutual fund that averages 12 percent annual growth, that $4,000 will grow to $1,566,333 tax free at age sixty-six. You realize you never added any money?!

Vision leads you to wealth. Vision is understanding that investing cable and pizza money of only $100 per month from age twenty to age sixty-five, your working lifetime will land you at retirement with $2,145,469. That is better than having to buy that cookbook *72 Ways to Prepare Alpo and Love It*. We have a retirement crisis in America today not from a lack of money, but from a lack of vision.

A lack of vision caused a lack of saving and then made it "normal" to take out loans—debt—for school. A lack of vision and therefore a lack of investing have saddled the average college graduate with over $15,000 in student loan debt. Of the seniors graduating from college this year 78 percent will have student loan debt. And while the principle the student owes may be $15,000, he will end up paying almost $22,000 with the interest on a typical student loan. If instead they or their parents had had vision they could have saved the money needed for college and avoided having the child start out in life in debt.

CHICKEN LITTLE LIVES ON

The lack of vision is so "normal" that people actually get mad at me and argue that the economy would collapse if we all stopped borrowing and started saving to pay cash for our purchases. This collapse idea is stupid, because to start with everyone would not become debt-free and stop borrowing at the same moment. A gradual move over the next decade is the most we could hope for, giving banking, car manufacturing, and housing time to adjust. As we stop wasting money paying credit card, car loan, and home-improvement loan interest, we'll have more money to actually buy real goods. At the point we all become debt-free the economy would explode, because a huge number of freed-up dollars would fuel a growth rate that would dwarf any house-of-cards growth rate that borrowed money could create.

REAL ESTATE ANIMALS

Vision not only causes you to choose between investing or spending, vision also makes you lucky. Real estate investing is where I see this "luck" tied to vision played out again and again. Dreamers, who buy real estate or order midnight cable TV tapes on how to get rich quick in real estate, will usually make large mistakes in their first investment or two. Dreamers also can be spotted as real estate investors who will buy anything. The dreamer has no plan except to make money, so he or she is open to every "great deal" that hits the market. Another animal in the real estate jungle is the speculator. This animal buys with hopes of cashing in on that perfect timing that they know is coming. The speculator is long on guts and short on research. The real estate speculator buys because of what the property should, could, would do in the next few months.

Almost twenty years ago, I got to watch as dreamers and speculators lost their shirts. The World's Fair was coming to town so everyone was going to get rich. Real estate was the way to capitalize on the rush of folks coming to the fair. First there would be a shortage of hotel rooms so even hundreds of miles away hotels were constructed. There was no shortage of rooms. Then there would be a parking crisis so forty miles away tobacco farmers were paving their fields. There was no parking crisis.

Greed isn't pretty. I have seen folks go crazy upon the announcement of a corporate headquarters or manufacturing plant coming to their area. They suddenly feel that their land is worth five times what it was yesterday. The sad thing is that there is a sucker born every minute, and some idiot will pay the price only to see prices settle back after the gold rush fever goes down.

The person who builds wealth with real estate is the person with vision. The real estate investor with vision buys in good neighborhoods at the far edge of a growth ring. The property might be a little green, not yet ripe for the picking. This type of investor will buy that small farm on the edge of town or the office building or apartment "out in the country." They buy and maintain property in good communities, and they are good for the community. Then ten or fifteen years later that property is right in the path of a major growth spurt and the visionary investor becomes wildly wealthy. The dreamer and the speculator both say, "Wasn't he lucky?" It wasn't luck, it was looking at things with the long-range planning window we call vision.

VISION CHANGES YOUR FAMILY TREE

If a sixteen-year-old can retire a millionaire, a working-class saver with $100 per month can retire a millionaire, and a visionary real estate investor can make a killing, what could you do? You could change your family tree! Tens of millions of dollars can be created as wealth for the next generations. What did the first Carnegie, Rockefeller, Vanderbilt, or Kennedy have when he started broke? Vision. Vision causes you to face your horizons without stopping, no matter how many times you fall.

Vision that is powerful enough to change a family tree is the noblest of traits. Several years ago, an older lady with a thick German accent called in on my radio show. She wanted to tell our listeners that saving and investing, as opposed to spending everything, works. She had come to America just following World War II as a widow with two young children. Can you imagine how popular Germans were in America just after the war? She didn't care, she had a vision. She came here with virtually no skills and worked over forty years as a seamstress. She also knew that she had to invest to achieve her vision. At the time she called me she was retiring, and on a seamstress's income she had paid for her home and had over $300,000 in mutual funds. Impressive? She also paid cash for both her children's college educations and gave them each enough to pay cash for their homes. I had to ask how she had sacrificed all that she obviously had, to achieve the goals she had. Her answer will stay with me forever: "Dave, when I came to America I had one goal—give my children a chance. I wanted to change my family's destiny."

How can you change your family tree? First you need to decide what it is that you want to accomplish. You might be thinking that you want to allow your child to attend college without creating debt. Or you might want to be able to show your children what living without debt allows you to accomplish today and in the future. Think about what you want to do to change your family tree and then read on, because vision must be put into practice.

THE MAGIC BEHIND THE VISION

Goals are the practical building blocks that make a vision come true. Goals are essential. The sad thing is that few people have goals and so few people convert their vision into action. One reason for this paralysis is past failures and fear of more failure. Alexander Graham Bell said, "When one door closes, another opens; but we often look so long and so regretfully upon the closed door that we do not see the one which has opened for us." It is much better to look where you are going than to see where you have been. Looking at past failures and mistakes to learn to avoid repeating them is smart. Too many people, however, have become navel gazers who are so caught up in self-analysis that they get nothing done. A driver using only the rearview mirror on his car will get nowhere fast. Look forward with vision and set bite-size goals to accomplish your vision.

Goals are where we put clothes on the vision and walk it down Main Street, USA. Goals that work must be four things:

1. They must be your goals, not someone else's idea or suggestion; you must own the goal.
2. They must be measurable. Convert your goal into a number so it is measurable. Measurability in money is all right if money isn't your only motivator. Try to measure your vision in something other than dollars.
3. Goals need to be written down. There is something powerful that God does for you when you force your thoughts onto paper. The writing process makes you clarify and take the goal into your gut.
4. All goals must have a time limit. Monthly, weekly, daily, or even yearly is fine but there needs to be a finish line.

Only about 8 percent of Americans have clearly defined goals and only 3 percent write them down. It is no accident that only 3 percent of Americans retire wealthy.

At our office, our team members are required to memorize and take into their gut our mission statement. They must chew it and swallow it down because our mission statement is the core vision of who we are. But we don't stop there. Every member of the team is required to have a personal mission statement that he writes down and which is kept in his personnel file. Once a team member has the company and personal vision set, then we require personal goals showing how he will play his vision out in the real world. So as you walk through our offices you will see numbers and dates on the walls by which we measure success, and you will see scripture and inspirational quotes that line up with the mission statements. Most of our team members will tell you that our team is the hardest place they have ever worked and yet the most fulfilling. I do not set goals for our team, ever. They set their own goals, and the passion that flows from their shared vision has created a team of people pulling together with an intensity that is incredible.

As a young salesperson I set goals for money and they were hollow. Money goals are a joke; they are no fun and not very motivating. Money is a selfish motivator and it will not keep you moving when the noonday sun burns bright on your forehead and you are looking for an excuse to quit. If you will develop goals that are outside yourself for serving others then those will translate to money. This level of nobility will motivate you when you need it. In our firm we measure sales in dollars, but we always discuss the goals in terms of numbers of families served. How many radio listeners do we have? How many books have helped folks? How many lives were changed at a seminar? If you measure success in service, money will flow to you in truckloads. Goals that flow from vision will make you hurt yourself working for them.

SHARE THE VISION

If you want your family to have More Than Enough, family goal setting is vital. In our culture of "me," having a shared vision and goals among husband, wife, and kids is a fun thing to watch. Our family struggles with balancing a very busy schedule: There is my son's softball, my daughter's soccer, our involvement in the church, my radio show and seminar schedule, and Sharon's PTO volunteer work. Yet with all the pulls on our individual time, we have maintained our sense of humor and have a great family because we work at shared goals. We have the shared goal to support each other in each of our activities. We also have the goal of finding ways as a family to serve others. Sharon cooks a meal for a shut-in and the kids deliver it with her. We enjoy one another's activities, I enjoy the ball games, and the kids work the book table at one of our seminars where they get to see people being helped. Whatever we do we are investing in one another with balance; that makes our "wild" life fun because we are always on one another's sidelines as cheerleaders.

TEACH YOUR CHILDREN

Children need to be taught goal setting early. Requiring nothing of a child gives them no opportunity for failure or success. Goal setting must be age-appropriate, however. Between ages three and nine the goals need to have very short time frames and be very reachable. Simply cleaning his room completely was a big deal for my four-year-old son. The hour he spent cleaning must have seemed like four days, but the satisfaction of a job well done made that four-year-old's chest stick out like he had just been elected president.

Examples of appropriate goals for young children ages three to nine are:

1. Doing an extra chore a week to save for the Toys "R" Them toy.
2. Giving their own money at the house of worship.
3. Skipping their favorite TV show for a few weeks to use the time to make family members birthday or Christmas gifts.
4. Blowing money on junk food or cheap toys as a reward.

Between the ages of nine and about fourteen, your children should begin to learn about vision and how goals flow from vision. By this age they can easily understand the basic division needed to divide the cost of the goal by the number of months until they plan to purchase the goal. This gives them the amount they need to save each month.

Then you can begin to show them how to set their own goals. As they learn to set measurable, written goals within set time frames you are building teens who don't fold to peer pressure. For example, your thirteen-year-old can establish some savings goals for short-term purchases as well as review the mutual fund statement with dad or mom to see how the college fund is coming. This gives them a look at short-term and long-term goals. How much babysitting or yard cutting equals a stereo purchase, and how much does a trip to the movies set you back from your goal?

IT IS CHILD ABUSE, NOT

Some of you may think that making children grasp that money is finite is mean. But what is really mean, bordering on child abuse, is to turn a child loose who doesn't know how to set and achieve goals and worse yet doesn't understand the life skill of saying no to the person in the mirror. Earl Nightingale said that the most important decision in achieving a goal is not what you are willing to do to achieve it, but what you are willing to give up to achieve it. The time to learn that lesson is between the ages of nine and fourteen and under the careful eye of a parent.

Some goals that a nine- to fourteen-year-old might have are:

1. Saving for a car purchase. If you can, match what they save; if you can't afford a 100 percent match, match the

amount you can afford so that they don't look to debt as the answer.

2. Continue to give at their house of worship.
3. They can save for more major purchases such as stereos or furniture, and then you have the opportunity to show them how to buy wisely.
4. Save for gift giving on holidays and birthdays.

As these cherubs bud into young adults the rope in goal setting must get longer. The parent's day-to-day involvement in the goal setting and progress reports along the way should be lessened. They will fall down, but so do you. Your job at this stage is to be more of an accountability partner to make sure that written measurable goals with time frames are set and met. More and more, the methods of achieving the goals must be left to the teen. At this age, the goals will reflect the passage these children are going through, from childhood into adulthood. Their goals should reflect that as well:

1. Planning car maintenance including tire replacement and insurance.
2. Making a breakdown of goals to allow funding for school trips, school rings, and other large-ticket items.
3. Teaching them to identify upcoming expenses further and further out.
4. Turn over their portion of the clothing budget completely to them with guidelines of what you allow them to purchase—you are still the parent.

Your children will not learn to set goals unless they see you setting and reaching your own goals and visions. When they see you setting goals they don't feel important and loved unless you are passing that skill to them. As important as it is that they understand what your visions are and how you plan to achieve them, it is also vital that you convey them in terms that are appropriate to your child's age. While a fifteen-year-old will understand that you have decided to forgo the expensive family vacation this year in order to save for his college fund, a five-year-old may not. It is also crucial that you and your spouse agree on what your goals and visions for the family are: The two of you should sit down together and write out your goals and visions; then you can use each other to keep on track as you work toward achieving them. If along the way, you have to make decisions to forgo something, the two of you should agree on that together and present a united front to your children when you explain to them why you won't be going to Disney World this year.

Goals make the difference. J.C. Penney said, "Give me a stock clerk with a goal, and I'll show you a man who will make history; give me a man without a goal and I'll show you a stock clerk." The rich do get richer and the poor do get poorer because of vision, and vision dressed in street clothes is called goals.

THE MAP AND COMPASS WILL
GET YOU THERE

The path to **MORE THAN ENOUGH** has directions. Your compass is your values; they lead you to the road, which is vision, and you are able to find your way using the road signs, called goals. There is victory only with vision. Your life will explode when you find a cause, a vision that motivates you beyond yourself. Dr. Martin Luther King, Jr., said, "If a man hasn't discovered something that he will die for, he isn't fit to live." When you wrap your arms around a vision for your life and that of your family, the goals will flow from that vision. You will then be on your way to changing your life and even your family tree. Go ahead, I dare you, stop and think again like you used to about what can be, instead of what was or should have been. Sit down today with your spouse and make a list of your visions for the future:

1. _____
2. _____
3. _____
4. _____
5. _____

And for each vision, write down the steps—goals—that you must achieve along the way:

1. My vision for my marriage is _____ and the goals I must reach are _____.
2. My vision for my children is _____ and the goals I must reach are _____.
3. My vision for my physical condition is _____ and the goals I must reach are _____.
4. My vision for my emotional state is _____ and the goals I must reach are _____.
5. My vision for my finances is _____ and the goals I must reach are _____.
6. My vision for my intellectual growth is _____ and the goals I must reach are _____.

Look boldly into your future and the future of your family and have the guts to make something of it.

THE STORY CONTINUES

Out of core **values, vision** is born. **Vision** is put into work clothes and becomes **goals. Vision** and its child, **goals,** are only effective and stand the test of time if they are born in **values.**

Thoughts from Sharon . . .

To me, having the vision of success means having goals and know-ing how to achieve them. Having a road map for your goals is a beginning. You need to set limits on what you want to accomplish within your lifestyle. Occasionally, I have to say no to some proj-ects, because if my platter gets too full, I'm not going to do a good job at the most important things. Goals and visions cannot be reached if you are not focused and are torn in a million different directions. I'm better at doing a few things and doing them well, rather than a lot of things and doing none of them very well.

Everyone should have their own goals and visions. Here's an example of a goal: Our oldest daughter, who is only thirteen, al-ready has a vision of her first car. Every time she sees a Mustang convertible going down the road she rejoices, because she sees that as her future "vision." That's just the beginning. Soon she will be setting goals for other things also.

Keys to the More Than Enough Mansion

1. Change is very hard and we change only when the pain of *same* is greater than the pain of change.
2. Cleansing cries and hinge pins are signals that we are ready.
3. Values really do matter and real values are the foundation of everything to come.
4. Integrity—real deep integrity, even with the little things—is vital because deception destroys.
5. Connectedness is key; take time to use the sidewalks that connect you to family, friends, and coworkers.
6. Vision that is rooted in values is the only vision that will last.
7. Vision makes you a long-term investor, not living for the moment.
8. Goals are the building blocks of vision, vision in work clothes.
9. Model for and teach your children about vision and goals.

4

The "You" in "Unity" Is Silent

O ne evening, after having spoken at a local church, I was approached by a man named Mike who asked if he could talk with me privately. When Mike, his pastor, and I sat in the pastor's study, he told the following story: Mike and Joan had gotten married against his family's wishes. His family is Greek and was upset that he was marrying an American. His dad told him it would never work because American women are too independent and he would never be the man of the house. Yet Mike and Joan had a good marriage and they had three beautiful children in eight years. As Mike told it, Joan was a "good woman"; She kept a clean home, she was a good mom, she was always cooking great meals, and yes, she did the bills. Joan was also always pushing Mike to make more of himself, to work more, and to take classes.

THAT'S WHAT FRIENDS ARE FOR

Then a friend of Mike's at work asked him to attend a meeting about a wonderful chance to make money. Mike went with his friend and was shown a multilevel company where if he worked really hard for three hours each week he could make $100,000 per year. There is nothing wrong with multilevel companies. They can be a dream come true, but you can't work three hours a week at anything and make $100,000 per year. Anyone who tells you that is lying.

Nonetheless, Mike joined up hoping his dreams would come true. After many weeks of hard work Mike had made no money and recruited no one, but he had spent $300 he and Joan didn't have on the company's products. Joan, while very supportive of Mike, began to recognize that this company was not what it claimed to be. She urged Mike to find something else to pour his skills and abilities into. When Mike told his friend about Joan's concerns the friend became very tense, telling Mike, "She is holding you back, as long as you have that woman you will never be successful."

Combined with his dad's negative view of Joan as well as the stress and responsibility of a wife and children, this new opinion caused Mike to separate emotionally from Joan. Mike then did one of the most stupid and short-sighted things that people can do: He found a younger girl at the office and began an affair. The affair led to a child out of wedlock and a separation from Joan. Mike ended up moving in with his dad.

While Joan is probably not the easiest woman to live with, Mike is at fault here. He has overlooked a vital principle: When you marry, you leave your father and mother; you cleave to your wife, forsaking all others. That vow means if your dad is a racist pig or a jerk to your mate then he can no longer be part of your life until he changes his behavior. That vow also means that if your "friend" puts down your mate then he should be punched, not listened to as wise counsel. Of all the people on the planet you should listen to, it is your mate. She has your best interest at heart, if for no other reason than she has to ride the wave with you. In listening to his father and to his "friend," Mike forgot that it is Joan, his wife, he is sharing his life with and that sharing a life with a spouse means creating unity.

THE "YOU" IN "UNITY" IS SILENT

Successfully married couples learn that the "you" in "unity" is silent. You win at marriage by losing your selfish need to get your way in every battle. I am not saying that you must be a doormat, but I am saying most of the turf that couples battle over isn't nearly as important as the damage the battle brings to the relationship. You get happy marriages by giving up selfish desires in order to win together—winning at creating your visions and goals that flow out of your shared values. This is the first part of the progression that will lead you to MORE THAN ENOUGH. If you and your spouse haven't yet sat down to discuss and write down your shared visions and the goals you must achieve to realize them, go back to chapter 3. Why? Because despite the fact that the preacher may have pronounced that "now you are one" you are not—except perhaps one construction project where you try to kill each other, especially during that first year of marriage. You remember those good fights, don't you? "Yeah and your mama's ugly too," those real fights where all the truth comes out. A lady recently called my radio show to tell me that in thirty-nine years of marriage she and her husband had never had a fight. Sure . . . and all the politicians in Washington are honest. I had to wonder if they lived in the same state. When we enter this brain-damaged state of mind called love, we think that if we just get married we can fix our mates and their habits. Wrong. The truth is, we come to marriage with our own value systems and ways of doing things; those values won't ever match our partner's without some work. And part of that work is learning how very different we are.

OPPOSITES ATTRACT

Sharon and I have three children under the age of thirteen, so we can lose our religion getting the family ready for church. I like to be on time and Sharon figures Jesus is already there so what's the rush. I am barking orders like Sergeant Carter on *Gomer Pyle* for teeth to be brushed and hair to be combed. Meanwhile a couple of my kids are acting like they are Gomer Pyle. Steve and Annie Chapman are friends of ours who minister to the family in churches across the world. With their perfect sense of humor they shared a similar story from stage one night and then Sharon used it on me the next Sunday. She told me on a stressful Sunday, "This Sunday why don't we trade places, you get the kids ready and I'll go out in the driveway and honk the horn."

UNDER CONSTRUCTION

The challenge in a marriage is to work through the different identities, ideals, and values you each bring to the relationship. It starts out innocently enough. At first you think, "Isn't it cute that he doesn't feel he has to be on time while I am so uptight." Later you are ready to kill him because he is always late for dinner. One of you is always hot and the other is freezing. When we were first married, Sharon and I had thermostat wars. The fights were so bad I threatened to get one of those locking covers so she would leave the temperature set. One of you enjoys crowds and the other wants a lonely walk on a deserted beach. The one who likes crowds is very bored on the deserted beach and doesn't understand why New York City brings stress. One of you organizes and the other has never folded a sock in his life. I am the nerd around our house, even my garage is clean! Sharon, while very clean and organized in her own way, is more of the creative type.

The very things that attract us to each other become the things that, if carried too far, can drive a wedge between us. Yet while our differences can frustrate us, we need each other because those differences are also strengths and allow us to cover each other's weaknesses. Larry Burkett of Christian Financial Concepts has a great saying which goes: "If two people just alike get married, one of you is unnecessary."

THE X AND Y CHROMOSOME FACTOR

Not only are our individual personality styles and tendencies different, we are also marrying someone of the opposite sex. This complicates things even further since men and women are different. Some fools in our society no longer believe that fact. But check with my very young son who took a bath with his very young sister, and he'll tell you they are not alike. Aside from the obvious plumbing differences, there are other substantial physical differences in muscle tissue percentages and fat percentages as well as in proteins and endorphins. Gary Smalley, the marriage counselor and author, explains that researchers have found that just prior to birth large amounts of chemicals release in the brain of baby boys creating what researchers call "brain wash." This "brain wash" literally damages a man's ability to focus on multiple tasks at the same time and explains why men are more single-task oriented while women are multi-tasked beings. That explains why we men can't hear her when the TV is on, and why she can cook, talk on the phone, and discipline the kids at the same time.

Dennis Rainey with the Family Life Marriage Seminar series tells couples that their research shows women are more verbal than men are. Men usually speak about 10 to 20,000 words per day while women speak 30 to 50,000 words per day with gusts up to 125,000. That is why many men don't feel like talking after work; they have used up their quota.

In Smalley's book, *Making Love Last Forever*, he lists five differences in male and female behavior that he has found through his research and years of counseling:

1. Men love to share facts, women love to express feelings.
2. Men connect by doing things, women connect by talking.
3. Men tend to compete, women tend to cooperate.
4. Men tend to be controlling, women tend to remain agreeable.
5. Men tend to be independent, women tend to be interdependent.

John Gray in his bestseller, *Men Are from Mars, Women Are from Venus*, describes men as having a sense of themselves that "is defined through his ability to achieve results. Men are preoccupied with the 'things' that can help them express power by creating results and achieving their goals." Of women, Gray says, "A woman's sense of self is defined through her feelings and the quality of her relationships. Instead of being goal oriented, women are relationship oriented; they are more concerned with expressing their goodness, love, and caring."

MONEY MAKES THE DIFFERENCES SHOW UP

When I tell audiences across America to have an emergency fund of three to six months of expenses saved in a simple money market account just for a rainy day I see these differences pop up. The relationship-oriented woman understands the need for an emergency fund not just in her head, but deep inside her instincts to protect the nest, and she wonders why her husband hasn't already done this. The man, on the other hand, can understand the emergency fund in his brain, but his task-oriented being won't let him leave it alone. Men say things like, "you want me to put $10,000 in a 5 percent account and just let it sit there when it could be in an investment at 12 percent, are you crazy?" The man wants to mess with the fund for every BBD (Bigger Better Deal) that comes along. We want to maximize the return, be efficient, leave the cave, kill something and drag it home. Guys, listen to me for just one minute. Because your lady is more relationship and security oriented than you are, she is smarter about this issue than you. Her nature leads her to better conclusions. When you set that fully funded emergency fund aside and she believes you won't touch it, she feels different, safer.

The best investment you will ever make is an investment in your marriage. By funding an emergency fund your wife will have her need for security met and you will even see her face relax as the stress leaves. Men, do this as a gift to your marriage, to your wife, not because she is weaker, but because she is wired differently. Men and women aren't equal, they are complementary.

SHOP TILL YOU DROP

Another area where the natural differences about money show up is in the area of shopping. Sharon and I read and attend seminars on marriage to constantly work at making our marriage better. We went to one seminar where the teacher did a wonderful job until he suggested that the men should express their love for their wives by shopping with them to spend quality time together. I don't know what planet he was from, but that is a crummy idea. I can do a six-hour seminar on my feet and not have my feet hurt, but about six minutes into a "shopping trip" my feet hurt to my neck. Gary Smalley describes a lame attempt like mine when he says men just don't get the shopping thing. We get out of the car at the mall and say, "Identify the target, we will map out the shortest distance through the mall to the store, grab the item, and find the fastest-moving or shortest checkout line. We will then kill the item and drag it to the car with maximum efficiency; let's synchronize our watches." The ladies are saying, "What are you talking about? You have to go to every store, touch everything in the store, and then learn about the clerk's family problems. We try on most everything, buy a lot of it, and then bring most of that back. This is an experience, a journey, not an assembly line." Being the dutiful husband that I am I decided to "improve my marriage" by going shopping with Sharon. Within twenty minutes I was outside on the little benches with all the other bald guys who must have gone to the same seminar; it didn't work.

Women get their deals by hunting, shopping, and shopping, and shopping. They will look until they find the perfect deal; time or effort don't enter into the equation because they enjoy the process. Men get good deals by negotiating; the warrior draws the sword, does battle over price and terms, and wins the victory. This process of the battle runs against a woman's nature of community and everyone being agreeable. The shopping trip runs against the man's nature of being task oriented. Neither is right or wrong, they are just different. We have learned to use these natural differences to win. Sharon hunts the deal down, comes home and tells me where it is, and I go kill it. There is a formula for MORE THAN ENOUGH.

WE ARE OPPOSITES WHEN IT COMES TO MONEY TOO

When it comes to money: Spenders attract savers. Most couples contain one spender and one saver and when they first wake up and realize they married "one of those," they freak out. The saver decides they will live on Kraft macaroni and cheese purchased, of course, with a coupon on double-coupon Thursday. The saver continues to lay down the law as to how they will save, save, save paper clips, coupons, yarn, even lint. They will live in a cave and never come out because that is the cheap thing to do. The spender does not hear the word "fun" anywhere here and begins to freak out: "I work hard and I deserve to live while I'm still alive." "Save money, what's that?" "My grandfather saved and didn't enjoy life, not me!" Of course this kind of speech confirms the saver's worst fear that he has married someone who is totally irresponsible. As a result, the saver immediately demands separate checkbooks and declares, "When we are old and you have spent all your money I might take care of you." The spender thinks separate checkbooks and finances are a great idea since this stranger he married is apparently allergic to fun. The spender will say something like, "Fine, you save, but when I am booking that seven-day cruise I'll see if there is room for you." They have that "discussion" and separate their finances and begin to financially operate like roommates instead of a married couple.

WHO IS REALLY IN CHARGE?

It isn't just how we spend money; it's also how we handle our finances that mark us as opposites. The mate with the administrative gift, the nerd, takes over the finances and falls under the illusion that he runs the show. The person handling the budget and bill paying could be either the man or the woman. In either case, the person doing the finances can, over time, feel resentful about having to shoulder the full weight of this responsibility. When resentment sets in, the bill-paying spouse begins to feel as though the mate is a large, dependent teenager who must be cared for. Meanwhile, the other mate doesn't necessarily feel cared for. Instead, this spouse may feel manipulated and controlled. The administrative person in your household may not be doing the bills if there has been some marriage stress over money already. You may have had that famous fight where one of you takes the box of bills, checkbooks, and budgets and throws it at your mate, yelling "You do it then!" in which case anyone, possibly even the cat, could be in charge of the finances.

THE NUMBER ONE CAUSE OF DIVORCE

Are you beginning to get the picture that this method, the equal but separate method, doesn't work? It is very sad that in most homes when mom or dad goes to balance the checkbook the kids hide in their rooms. The stress around the area of money in the family is incredible; our differences and the lack of a good plan of attack bring it on. *Worth* magazine did a detailed survey and found that the number one thing American married couples fight about is money. *USA Today* published the results of a study done for the Lutheran Brotherhood that shows that when we fight about money we fight most about the use of credit, shopping and spending, and then budgeting. Don't you love studies that show what we already know? *Jet* magazine published an article called "Why Money Is the Leading Cause of Divorce," which refers to a study by Citibank showing that 57 percent of divorces are caused by money problems. Scripps Howard news service is quoted in *The Detroit News* as saying that "statistics show that as many as 70 percent of divorcing couples attribute the breakdown of their marriages to arguments over money." Money problems destroy marriages and so does having a marriage without shared visions and goals.

WORKING AS A DUO

Bob and Sue, a blue-collar couple, had been married for eight years. Their marriage was on the rocks over money problems. Sue had been doing the finances and had become very bitter because of shouldering all the responsibility and stress. She felt abandoned in a storm and was making comments like, "I just wish he would act like a man and take responsibility."

Bob is a great guy with a heart the size of all outdoors, where he spent much of his time. Bob liked to deer hunt, fish, camp, and a lot of other things many of us enjoy. He was spending tons of money on these recreational hobbies and had no idea that the amount of money was unreasonable based on their income. All he knew was he worked hard so he thought that gave him the right to play hard. After all, "mama" was good with the money stuff. There were some long fights. Sue had become a nag because of her frustration and fear; so every time Bob went near a fishing pole everything would blow up and he had no idea what he had done. Their love made them able to give up defending their own turf, to see that the "you" in unity had to be silent in order to work through their money problems. He recognized that shouldering Sue with all the responsibility was not a compliment, but a cop-out. They began doing a budget together, which allowed them to share the stress and, later, the opportunity that their money brought them. As they shared the development of their monthly budget, Bob was able to include his hobbies without destroying the household finances because he now had some perspective. I don't know if I have ever seen a woman love a man as much as the night Bob decided after looking over their budget that he should sell his most prized possession, his set of handmade fly rods. "After all," Bob said, "It's just stuff." And as it turned out, Sue wasn't opposed to a good fishing trip herself; they actually began to do some of these things together, or Bob was able to go at Sue's urging rather than having to sneak off. It is amazing what sharing burdens, sharing goals, communicating, and doing a budget together can do. So guys, what we are saying is that budgets done together equal no-nag fishing trips, a small prize to pay for greatness.

IT IS TEST TIME

How much do you know about your family's finances? If you are the spouse who lets "mama" (or "papa" for that matter) handle the purse strings you need to get involved and start asking some questions. Later in this chapter, we'll walk through how you and your spouse will budget together, but for now try these questions on for size:

1. What is our monthly income?
2. How much a month do we spend on food, gas, or kids clothes?
3. Do we have money invested or saved anywhere?
4. Is handling all the bill paying stressful for you?
5. Can I help?

Remember to ask these questions in a spirit of cooperation and love. You aren't trying to interrogate your spouse, you're trying to get involved.

WHEN ONE OF YOU IS AN "EXPERT"

Jack and Sonja came to our Financial Peace offices for small business counseling and so Jack could get one of our financial counselors to tell Sonja just "how it is." Jack is an entrepreneur with a strong personality and knows a lot more about money than Sonja, so he believed she should just follow his excellent advice. The only problem was that his advice was always to do what he wanted and seldom what she wanted. Their relationship was folding fast; she had put up with ten years of his bullying and manipulating, and even though Sonja was a shy, laid-back person she was through taking it.

Jack brought her to counseling so she would get back in line, and I don't think he bargained for what he got. We advised this couple to begin marriage counseling immediately and attend one of our "small group" financial seminars. When it came time for Jack and Sonja to do a budget together, Jack was "just too busy." One night, I sat in the group and watched as Sonja tried to explain the pain and the hurt that his controlling her with money was bringing. The pain of ten years showed clearly in her eyes. Then as Jack said he was too busy, too smart, too important to budget and agree on spending with his mate several of the ladies in the group tore into him. For the next few minutes these she-bears took him out to the woodshed, and when he tried to get up several of the men took up the fight. These were men who had also been resistant and who now were enjoying the benefits of agreed spending. After a few minutes, I pulled the mob off of poor Jack. He was only slightly bruised in the ego, but he had a new look of understanding on his face. No, Jack didn't become a wimp that night, he became a man. He burned off some of the selfishness that had been controlling his life and turning him into a manipulator. My guess is that night, Jack heard and saw the importance of shared goals for the first time in ten years of marriage—and taking the lesson to heart, he can count on at least another ten years of marriage to Sonja.

ANOTHER TEST: ARE YOU PASSING?

You're "in charge" of your family's finances, but I bet you don't think Jack's story applies to you. Well, even if your personality is less strong than Jack's, you are manipulating your spouse if you agree with two or more of the following statements:

1. When it comes to investing, I choose the amount, the timing, and place we invest our money.
2. I pay all the bills.
3. When it comes to tax time, I only want my spouse to sign on the dotted line.
4. I haven't been exactly clear about how much money I really earn.
5. I have all the household bills sent to me at the office so that my spouse doesn't have to worry about them.
6. The thing is, I'm really interested in finances, and my spouse isn't—what's the problem?

The problem is that you probably aren't being honest, you certainly aren't giving your spouse a voice in the kind of life you will have together, and you're being manipulative.

THE "INDEPENDENT" WOMAN

Sally and Leo faced a different view of the same problem. Sally had decided that since she was a professional woman with an excellent income that she should be an "independent" woman. She had grown up in a home with an overbearing father who controlled every move, emotion, and dollar her mother ever thought of having. Sally, like any intelligent and gifted person, rebelled against the oppression of her upbringing. Her promise to herself to never be under any man's thumb the way her mother was made her a strong and self-sufficient woman, but was also damaging her relationship with her loving husband Leo. Unlike Sally's father, Leo was a nurturing and supportive husband who was proud of her accomplishments and as a successful small businessman was not the least bit threatened by Sally's success. The wound from childhood caused Sally's fierce independence, and despite Leo's love and support they were growing apart instead of together. Sally was sure if she combined finances with her husband that she would fall under his control and lose her identity.

THE WAY OUT

My challenge to Sally and the idea that finally enabled her to get past that fear was for her to just try a trial run. Just try to run things together for ninety days, and if Leo transformed into her father from the loving nurturing guy that he was, she could always go back to her own checkbook. Of course being the great guy that he was Leo didn't become a troll, and slowly Sally's fear was removed and replaced with respect and a new level of fondness for Leo and oneness in her marriage. Of course when we started talking about all this Sally was very philosophical and political in her defense of the "independent" position. As it turned out she wasn't so political as she was just wanting a fair playing field with the man she loved.

If you want to be an independent woman that is fine, but don't get married. Separating your money in the name of independence robs you of the unity and oneness that great marriages have. Separating your money puts you in the spiritual and emotional position of separation: You remember, what you do right before divorce. Marriage doesn't mean you lose your identity or competence, it does mean you have brought someone into your life you would die for. You have to die all right, die to self.

Do you and your spouse have separate finances? Separate checking and savings accounts, separate mutual funds, separate retirement accounts? If you do, list the reasons you've decided to separate your finances below:

1. _____
2. _____
3. _____
4. _____
5. _____

Now, I can't and don't know your individual circumstances, but I'm willing to bet that at the root of most of your reasons is fear: fear of being controlled, fear that the marriage won't last, fear that you'll somehow lose your identity if you loosen your stranglehold on your "own" money. Baloney. Most of the reasons for separation of money have to do with power, priorities, fear, or a misunderstanding of the natural differences you bring into the marriage. None of those things will happen if you and your spouse work through your fears and the finances together.

THE BLENDED FAMILY

Are you and your spouse still dickering over the mine, yours, and ours in your blended family? This situation presents particular problems, as I've said before. In order to resolve them you have to do some hard work to deal with the many agendas and issues from the past that project into the present. You need a plan that will give you and your spouse much more unity. First, if you haven't thought through your values and goals go back to chapter 2; sit down with your spouse and create a plan that the two of you agree upon. Second, work through your budget together (see page 308 for guidelines). Then if there are teens in your family, I suggest you have them sign off on the budget. When the teens or mature pre-teens understand the overall goals of the family as reflected in the budget, they are more ready to accept the limitations. The limitations, when seen as part of a whole, are perceived as logical, and the kids don't get the impression that they are Cinderella being persecuted by the evil stepparent. Unity brings peace to any household.

REAL BOY SCOUT KNOTS ALWAYS HOLD

Dennis Rainey, noted marriage author, counselor, and radio host, says we get married with two sets of blueprints to build a house. One of you has a plan for a ranch and the other mate has a plan for a trilevel. If you don't sit down and make some adjustments you will build a pretzel. Many of you have. Solo is not the way to be married, duo is. We cannot run the sound system on mono, but only in stereo, where we get full use of our differences working in concert. The tweeters and the woofers when working together make some beautiful music.

So who should be doing the financial decision making? Both, both, both of you. This is not a joint venture; it is a marriage, and a peace will come with your joint decisions. Larry Burkett says money is either the worst area of communication in a marriage or the best. I tend to think it is both in part because of all the differences we bring to the budgeting and finance table.

I have told you that opposites attract. Usually one of you is more creative and spontaneous. That mate is a little or even a lot less organized and tends to see budgeting as a form of torture or a method of the other mate controlling her. That describes Sharon. The other mate has more administrative skills and more of a bent toward numbers; there lives deep inside of this mate a nerd. That describes me. The nerd can be the man or the woman, and believe it or not the nerd can be the spender or the saver. Pain has taught me to live otherwise, but my nature is the spender while Sharon is the tightwad. Normally if one of you has all the budgeting responsibility it is the spouse with the administrative bent. The nerd gets the budget because he is the only one who cared and couldn't trust anyone else anyway since he is so smart. The nerd then will do this seventeen-page perfect budget and present it to the family like a gloating benevolent dictator. The subjects all bow in appreciation and then go do whatever they want with the money. This unauthorized flow of money upsets the nerd, and further controls are implemented; at which time the free spirit will dig in his heels and the budget wars are on. I have just described, maybe overstated, maybe not, how most couples "manage" money.

GOOD, BETTER, BEST

There is a better way. Years of counseling and small groups have helped us develop a system that works. When I developed this program, I thought it was to force couples to control their spending, but one of the byproducts is shared values and saved marriages. This observation about marriage is the most unexpected and thrilling discovery about this program. Here's how it works: First, the nerds should prepare the budget, because we love to, it is our life. Instead of making the budget kingly law we should submit it to the budget committee. The budget committee is the two of you. The budget committee has rules. Nerds, you are on my team, and free spirits, you are on Sharon's team. Nerds, when you submit your masterpiece budget to the committee you must remember to shut up and listen. Free spirits will not come to any more meetings if the meeting consists of your telling them what they are going to do and how smart you are for having figured it out. By doing the first draft of the budget you have had your say. Now listen and accept the fact that your mate has valid input and agree to most of the requested changes. You are doing this to bribe your spouse into the process of managing money, and believe me your concessions are a small price to pay for unity.

KEEP IT SHORT, SILLY

The meeting must be short; this is a budget committee meeting not a Camp David accord. Nerds like me love to look at all possible scenarios and do projections and pro formas. We can make Quicken a hobby. Nerds, when your objective is agreement with your free spirit you need to remember you have about a seventeen-minute window of opportunity before they leave. They may be physically sitting there, but their minds left and went on to non-nerd activities that are more important to them. Nerds, your three rules for the budget committee meeting are:

1. Listen.
2. Take input.
3. Keep it brief.

RULES FOR THE OTHER SIDE

Free spirits, you must show up for the budget committee meeting. Yes, this activity is important to your marriage, your children's future, and the only way you can defend your position is to come to the meeting. Free spirits, you must clean up your language. There is a phrase you can never again say. No matter what happens the rest of your life you may never again utter these words: "Whatever you want to do, honey." Wrong, cop-out breath, you have to stick in there and make this work. And as you sit there, you must be a grown-up and realize that we cannot spend more than we make and have financial security or build wealth. Your wants, needs, and desires must be combined with your family's and the new total must be less than your family income. Free spirits, your three rules are:

1. Show up.
2. Give input.
3. Be realistic.

The purpose of the budget committee meeting is to spend every dollar of income for the upcoming month on paper and agree with your mate on every single item in the budget. Income minus outgo must equal exactly zero—every dollar has a name. I don't care what you assign your dollars to, but you must give every dollar a name. If you have never put a budget together, you can use the sample forms on pages 308–311 as a model. New budgets will require frequent maintenance. The first month you will have to have weekly emergency budget committee meetings to adjust for errors and to re-zero your plan. You must not spend money ever, except as is on the plan; so if you don't like the plan adjust it, but only with both of you agreeing to the changes. Your first three months won't work well and you will have to have several emergency budget committee meetings to adjust for when life happens. The fun thing is over time your accuracy for life as reflected in a plan will get so good that budgeting will become second nature.

THE BEST MARRIAGES DO IT

Remember, when you have agreed on the next month's budget you are setting goals *together* that flow from your vision, which is based on your values. When you and your spouse agree on all these things—values, vision, and goals combined—you don't give up your individual identities, you add to them. You are forced to agree on your passions, priorities, dreams, fears, and yes, that all flows from your value system. If you agree on spending, you have been forced to do the hard marital work and communication it takes to meld your separate value systems into one. If you overcome your sex and personality differences through communication and achieve a shared value system, you will reach a level of unity in your marriage that most only dream about. The forcing of shared checking accounts and budgets has healed more failing marriages and taken more lackluster marriages back into fabulous passion than any other marriage technique. The level of unity, oneness, and the resulting return of communication and romance that sharing your finances can bring to a marriage cannot be overstated. In fact, it is truly the way that you and your spouse, probably for the first time in your marriage, become one. Budgeting together, spending together on paper first forces you to make the "you" in unity become silent.

DON'T LOOK BACK

When you achieve this wonderful unity that I keep harping about you will never want to go back. Sharon and I use money and time as major points of communication. We have found that if we will be courteous to each other about the budget and the calendar we win. We also plan together using these two tools and that enables us to manage a very busy life with very little disagreement. We have rules: We do not change the budget or the calendar without agreement. Sometimes agreement is a simple phone call. We do not buy items over $300 without talking first.

OH THOSE FEELINGS

I am the financial person and Sharon is not. You can imagine my surprise several years ago to discover that she had an opinion. Then I was really shocked that not only did she have input, but also that it was frustratingly always right. When she gets one of those "feelings" I hate it, but I have learned to trust it. With all my finance degrees and business ability I never saw the need to heed Sharon's input until I went broke and was broken. Pride is a dangerous thing. Now ten years after losing everything I am very willing to hear her, not because I am weak, but because I am strong enough to know better. Before we make major decisions at our company Sharon is brought in to meet the players and see what her "feeling," her insight is. Sharon is a full-time mom; but before anyone goes to work full-time for our firm she interviews him and we both interview his spouse. Some folks think that is extreme; but we have tremendous productivity and unity within our team and Sharon's insight is part of the reason. She also attends all of our managers' meetings, which are held once a week. Her wisdom and insight are legendary in our company. As one of our newer team members said the other day, "I thought she would be taller."

John Gray says women have developed this "women's

intuition" through centuries of anticipating the needs of others. I am not sure about that. I tend to believe that a lady's special feel for "things" is a gift of God, it is the way she is designed, and marvelously so. Proverbs 31:10–11 says, "Who can find a virtuous wife? For her worth is far above rubies. The heart of her husband safely trusts her: So he will have no lack of gain." Men, that is a financial principle that will lead you toward MORE THAN ENOUGH. Men who listen to virtuous wives will have "no lack of gain." Men, listen to your wives.

Ladies, the verse said virtuous, not a mad terrier barking around his ankles. To command the level of respect I am speaking of requires that you put others' interests ahead of your own and that you reason with maturity.

IT'S NEVER TOO EARLY TO START

A listener from Mississippi sent an E-mail to our radio show, sharing a valuable lesson:

> I'm sure that you have touched on this subject before, but I believe that it is a message that cannot be repeated enough. I'm a thirty-six-year-old widowed father of two. Two years ago my wife and children's mother was lost to an auto accident. At that time, I was a typical bread-winning male. I worked very hard and made a very good living. I was able to provide a comfortable living for my family and was content in doing that. I left the bill paying

and most of the financial matters to my wife. Even though she asked for my help and input a lot, I was always able to wear her down and get out of it. When she passed away I was a lost little puppy. I couldn't even find the checkbook, much less find insurance policies, unpaid bills, etc. Needless to say life was rough. I'm sure I don't need to tell you what kind of emotions are going through someone who has just lost a life partner.

I would give anything to be able to go back and share more with my wife. Paying bills and balancing checkbooks with my wife would be a lot of fun now. I missed out on that, but I hope other men will heed the warning and get more involved with the day-to-day operation of their home. I feel like I cheated myself and my wife out of an important part of our relationship. I can't go back and correct that, but I can warn others that there are definitely no guarantees. When you loose your partner, it's over. So don't take them for granted and make sure you enjoy them while you have that valuable time.

Please reach with intensity for this unity while you can. By putting the lessons in this chapter into practice and storing them deep within your heart you will revolutionize your marriage and your money. Start today:

1. What are the differences between you and your spouse that frustrate you? How would your spouse respond to this question?
2. Pick one habit that you think annoys your spouse and *stop* doing it.

3. The next time you discuss finances with your spouse, try assuming your spouse's point of view.
4. Sit down with your spouse and create your budget.
5. As you're talking about your budget, allow yourselves to dream about the future: What would you like to have your money working toward?

This process will take time, but in case you haven't figured it out I believe with every ounce of my heart that achieving unity between the two of you and in your finances is more than worth it. If you learn to make the "you" in unity silent, your marriage and your money will land you in the MORE THAN ENOUGH column.

THE STORY CONTINUES

Out of core *values, vision* is born. *Vision* is put into work clothes and becomes *goals.* Shared *goals* give you *unity* with those who are on the journey with you.

Thoughts from Sharon . . .

Dave says the "you" in "unity" is silent, and I'll add the U in "communications" is essential.

Communication is the key to a strong marriage. I learned the hard way, because for so long I was the U in unity . . . I was silent.

In a marriage each partner should learn to stop and listen to his spouse, even if that is hard to do. Each of you has to express your views to each other no matter what. If you're quiet like I used to be, plan ahead when you feel strongly about something. Prepare yourself so you can really say what's on your mind without backing off if your spouse objects. And if you're better at talking than listening, make yourself stop and think about what's being said before you open up with your opinions. Both of your opinions count. But each of you must learn to be patient and really listen to the other and help each other say what's on your minds.

The key result of open communication and unity is a long, happy, and stronger marriage that helps to build your maturity level and trust with your spouse.

Keys to the More Than Enough Mansion

1. Change is very hard and we change only when the pain of *same* is greater than the pain of change.
2. Cleansing cries and hinge pins are signals that we are ready.
3. Values really do matter and real values are the foundation of everything to come.
4. Integrity—real deep integrity, even with the little things—is vital because deception destroys.
5. Connectedness is key; take time to use the sidewalks that connect you to family, friends, and coworkers.
6. Vision that is rooted in values is the only vision that will last.
7. Vision makes you a long-term investor, not living for the moment.
8. Goals are the building blocks of vision, vision in work clothes.
9. Model for and teach your children about vision and goals.
10. Opposites attract and men and women are different; identify and admit those differences and use each other's strengths for More Than Enough.
11. Men, build an emergency fund and leave it alone; it will change the way your wife treats you.
12. Budgeting together brings tremendous oneness to your marriage, but you must die to selfishness; the "you" in "unity" must be silent.

5

Hope: Balm for the Soul

When I was a teenager my family moved from the suburbs out to "the country." Mom and Dad bought several acres and we city kids started playing out our own version of *Green Acres*. My sister, Barbara, decided she was a cowgirl and joined the high school rodeo team. Dad bought her a horse to barrel race in competition. She also decided that she would enter another event. In fact, she decided that she was going to become a world champion goat roper.

So we bought her a goat to practice with and we named him "Practice." With Barbara atop her horse, her rodeo friends would give Practice a boot to get him running. Sis would ride after Practice, lasso him, and tie off the rope on the saddle horn. Practice would still be running while the horse had stopped, and about the time the rope ran out Sis would arrive. As Practice's neck popped she used the momentum to flip Practice upside down and then tie his feet together. The first time or two Practice was turned loose, you could just tell he thought, "I'm going to be free,

I'm not a goat, I'm a gazelle." No goats aren't known for being real bright, but after having his neck popped and being flipped upside down at about the same spot in the field several hundred times in the Tennessee summer heat, ole Practice began to catch on. He finally got to the point where he would run out to that spot in the field and stop. He even reached the point where he would run out to that spot, stop, and then lay down. We told Barbara that if we could get him to tie his own feet she could win every rodeo.

What happened to Practice? At first he thought he was a gazelle, then life happened. After life happened enough he began to believe that failure was all there was, so he stopped. Practice lost his hope.

HOPE IS A POWERFUL FUEL

You will never have **MORE THAN ENOUGH** unless you plug into one of the most powerful traits that we humans can possess: hope. Hope is the powerful fuel that causes the engine of your life to develop all the horsepower it was designed to have. Values that bring vision and unity will always be put into motion when hope comes on the scene. Hope creates motion.

I used to think, "cute," when someone mentioned the word hope. I made the mistake of thinking of hope as a sissy word with flowers and valentines around it. After years of watching folks get **MORE THAN ENOUGH** I have realized that hope is one of the most powerful things that can or cannot happen in someone's life. Hope is steel covered in velvet. It can seem soft and cuddly, but hope is the core of what makes people become what God designed them to be. Hope and its sister, faith, always create action.

HOPE MOVES US

Patrick Overton's statement shows how hope pushes us forward: "When we walk to the edge of all the light we have and take that step into the darkness of the unknown, we must believe that one of two things will happen, there will be something solid for us to stand on or God will teach us how to fly." Hope moves us forward when logic and energy are gone. Hope is a motivator.

If hope is a mover then we can easily see that a lack of hope causes us to stop. When hope is gone we quit. Where there is no hope paralysis sets in and we freeze up with apathy. Proverbs 13:12 says, "Hope deferred maketh the heart sick. . . ." When you lost hope your heart becomes sick and you lose the energy to make your vision become a reality. When folks come to us for financial counseling who are neck deep in debt and feel like they are fighting a losing battle, we see the early signs of depression. They tend to sleep late; they just don't have the energy to fight the day. They don't want to write down a spending plan; they say, "It's no use, I'm not going to make it." When Sharon and I were losing everything, we felt like

there was no light at the end of the tunnel but an oncom-
ing train. We felt like we didn't have the energy to fight another day, but one day my wise mother called and said,
"They can take everything, but the only way you lose your
hope is you have to surrender it." Hope is an act of the
will, it is a decision.

IS FAILURE PERMANENT?

As I have walked with thousands of families through
hope-robbing financial problems, I have realized there
are reasons that we lose our hope. Our mind and spirit
have to believe lies in order to lose that most precious
item called hope. One big hairy lie that we allow to steal
our hope is: Failure is permanent. If we see failure in our
past as an indicator of our future, our only possible future,
that will rob our hope. Winston Churchill, the great Brit-
ish prime minister, said, "Success is going from failure to
failure without loss of enthusiasm." When we believe failure is here to stay we lose enthusiasm and the ability to
head back toward success. Hope is stolen when we mis-
understand failure. Failure is natural, normal, and is going
to happen. The way to reach **MORE THAN ENOUGH** is to keep
failure in its cage. Failure is caged when we realize it is not
permanent. Steel cages that hold failure in its proper view
are strong enough to stack on top of one another. Caged
failure is a building block. If we take all the lessons
learned from failure and stack them we can easily get the

breathtaking view that hope gives. Henry Ford, who definitely had **MORE THAN ENOUGH**, said, "Failure is the opportunity to begin again more intelligently." The trick is to avoid making short-term decisions, based on a loss of hope, that have worse long-term effects.

When people are in financial difficulty they often make stupid short-thinking financial decisions. If you really believe you can never save enough money to pay cash for a car, you lose hope and borrow the money. Debt, which robs your ability to build wealth, is usually the result of lost hope. We have been sold debt so thoroughly that it has stolen our hope. People who have hope, grown from vision based in values, are savers and investors; they think long term. Where there is a lack of hope we cripple our ability to build wealth and long-term relationships of value.

HOW DO YOU GET UP?

Loss of hope from being gut punched one too many times can happen to any of us. What causes some people to be able to get up again while others can't seem to find the energy? Someone once asked Paul Harvey, the radio commentator, to reveal the secret to his success. "I get up every time I fall down," was Harvey's answer. Vince Lombardi said, "It is not whether you get knocked down, it is whether you get up." The folks who get up again and again and keep going until they get **MORE THAN ENOUGH** from life are the folks who do not accept failure as destiny. Instead, they are always reminding themselves that failure is not an indicator of the future, but just a building block to get there. Dale Carnegie believed that when he said, "Develop success from failures. Discouragement and failure are two of the surest stepping stones to success."

FAILURE IS NOT PERMANENT

Not long ago it was time for my six-year-old son's training wheels to come off and make that step toward adulthood, learning to ride a bike. The Saturday morning weather was perfect, so we sent his sisters and mom shopping so the guys could take on this rite of passage together. Off came the training wheels, on came the look of fear. He had seen the other kids ride, but could he? I got my running in trying to make sure he didn't fall while also trying to give him room to balance and build confidence. Once, he got too far away and fell, scraping his hands and of course the knee. Through the tears I saw betrayal in those brown eyes: "Dad, you said you'd catch me!" Like any good parent I knew that I had to give him room to fail or he couldn't grow and learn. The trick to being a good bicycle riding coach is never let the student look at the failure as permanent. So after some dinosaur Band-Aids we went back to the bike, and after more practice and failure he is now an old pro. We adults all chuckle to ourselves when our children experience failure that seems so overwhelming to them. In our wisdom we know they will ride the bike, they will get another date, they will get another time at bat, and they will succeed if they just don't quit. Why don't we remember that wisdom when life deals us a blow?

THE PAST IS JUST THAT—PASSED

Walt Kallestad in his great book on leadership, *The Everyday, Anytime Guide to Christian Leadership*, says, "Relentless hope creates energy, to hope is to be able to cope." When past failure sneaks up and steals our hope we must have been mentally asleep at the wheel because we know better, realizing that failure is part of the process. There is a great scene in *The Lion King* that reminds us to keep the past in its place. Rafiki, the witch doctor monkey, has found the prince of the jungle, Simba, who is in hiding. Why is he hiding? Because of what he wrongly believes he did in the past. Simba refuses to go back to his kingdom to take his rightful place as king because of his past. At this point Rafiki takes his walking stick and violently hits the young lion prince on the head. Simba, shaking his head in pain, yells, "What was that for?" Rafiki wisely answers, "It doesn't matter; it is in the past. The past can hurt, but you can either run from it or learn from it."

Have you done something stupid or wrong in the past that you are still reliving daily? Is that memory haunting you and stealing your hope and your destiny? Maybe we can all take a lesson from something as silly as this cartoon: The past only has power over you if you give it that power. The past can hurt, but you can either run from it or learn from it.

A WEAK FOUNDATION WILL ALWAYS CRUMBLE

When you place your hope on the wrong things they will hurt you, bruise you, and probably steal your hope. Remember your first big job? That job was with the best company, it had the best growth potential, and best of all it had geniuses for managers. Then you showed up for work and after less than a month you discovered that people worked at this company. Flawed people worked there and, worse yet, flawed people ran the company.

For those who are married, do you remember when you first realized you were in love? Wasn't that future mate just the most fabulous thing on earth? After less than a month of marriage, you discovered that this person had some horrible habits. After ten years of marriage you discovered some of those horrible habits could even become character traits. Some folks can't recover from the shock that Prince Charming or Sleeping Beauty is human after all and even go so far as to divorce.

But surely you can place your hope in a church, can't you? Well, I made a discovery about churches long ago: They have people in them, sometimes really flawed people. Some churches even have pastors who aren't perfect! I know that revelation is shocking, but you wouldn't believe the number of folks who quit worshiping God because there are flawed people around the process.

STUFF NEVER EQUALS HAPPINESS

When we place our hope in stuff, we are frequently let down. Your brain should tell you that stuff does not equal happiness, and yet many folks collect more, bigger, and better stuff. There is no end to collecting stuff when you place your hope of happiness on stuff. You will never have a new enough car, a large enough china cabinet, or a fast enough boat, because every time you get home with it you are disappointed to find that someone has a better car, a bigger china cabinet, a faster boat. Then the stuff breaks, which adds to the heartbreak. Placing hope on stuff doesn't work either.

Financially, placing your hope on the wrong things will make you broke and keep you broke. If your hope is placed on stuff, you will buy, buy, buy in an effort to get "there," wherever "there" is. Most of the time this searching for happiness in stuff is a subtle process. Virtually no one says to themselves, "I will find happiness in stuff, I will place my hope in stuff." Few folks would be that immature and stupid. Instead this process of misplaced hope happens one item at a time. I'll be happy when I get that _____ (you fill in the blank). And yet when you finally get that _____, you haven't found the happiness you'd thought you would and the cycle starts all over again. All too often this "stuffitis" leads to debt or a lack of savings.

Then when the financial problems hit, we again find that men and women experience them differently. I have already told you that money problems are the number one cause of marriage problems and divorce. How can that be prevented and the problems headed off? We can start by understanding the differences in male and female reactions to financial stress.

BOYS AND THEIR TINKERTOYS

Men use money as a scorecard. Money is a measuring stick to see whether we are successful. Since we are more single-minded and task oriented than women, we take the chase for money very seriously. When money problems hit the scene we also take that as a direct indication of personal failure. If the scorecard says we are short then we must have lost, so money problems really affect men's self-esteem. The knight in shining armor is forced to notice that there is a chink in the armor, which is very painful. This loss of self-esteem is very real and can be dangerous: The number one cause of male suicide is financial problems, while almost no female suicides are financially based.

Men are problem solvers, and if we don't have an answer we get really scared. In his book *Men Are from Mars,*

Women Are from Venus, John Gray says, "A man is most uncaring when he is afraid." Men go into survival mode and can steamroll anyone or anything that gets in the way when they are scared. If you are facing tough financial times, the man in your life may be acting more like an adolescent than at any time you have known him. While he does not need false praise he does need positive reminders that you are not with him because of *what* he does or earns, but you are there because of *who* he is. Criticize a man in financial difficulty and you will see instant and dramatic flight or fight. He needs his armor shined and his sword sharpened, not a Chihuahua barking around his ankles reminding him of all past failure.

GIRLS AND THEIR BARBIES

As I told you earlier women are more relationship and security oriented, so financial problems attack them in those areas. While men lose self-esteem, ladies experience fear on a level men cannot comprehend. Because this need for security is a deep need and is at stake when the house payment is behind, a lady will have a level of fear that my wife says can approach terror. In one of our financial seminars, Betty, a fifty-six-year-old mother of four, described the feeling well:

> I feel like I am driving seventy miles per hour down the interstate and hit a large patch of ice. The car starts to

spin out of control, spinning left, then to the right, completely out of control. Time seems to slow down and I can't find air to scream with. I know we are going to hit something and hit it hard. I just can't tell what we are going to hit or when, so it is hard to brace myself. I feel that kind of terror with foreclosure, repossession, garnishment, and maybe even bankruptcy facing us. I feel so helpless.

Betty sums it up pretty well, doesn't she? How do we manage these normal feelings in bad financial times?

John Gray gives some insight when he reminds us, "Men feel better solving problems, while ladies feel better by talking about problems." Guys, if you are struggling financially, the lady in your life doesn't need to hear your plans or strategies as much as she needs to talk about relationships and she needs security reassurance. I am not saying you should deceive or hide the awful truth because she is too fragile. On the contrary, she is probably more resilient than you are right now, but she is wired differently. While I am asking her not to nag and instead to shine your armor, you guys have two things you need to do. One, don't retreat and clam up, she needs to talk. Even though talking might be hard for you, communication will save your marriage. Assignment number two, she needs four to ten good nonsexual hugs per day for reassurance. Some of you guys don't know what a nonsexual hug is and maybe it is time to learn. Reassurance not that the money problems are going to be solved overnight, but that no matter what happens you will be there and "we are staying together."

AH, TO BE YOUNG AGAIN, NOT!

Some of the most vicious people we have encountered in our years of financial counseling are twenty-somethings with financial problems. They are not vicious to outsiders, but to their mates. The first few years of marriage are about becoming one, which is a gut-wrenching process of giving up "rights." Ladies find out that he is not a knight in shinning armor or a Ken doll that does everything he is told. Men find out that she can't cook like Mama and to our horror she is not our maid either. I have one friend who says when he and his wife first got married he knew it was time to eat when the smoke alarm went off. Add to that normal stress the fact that the young couple buys a bunch of stuff they can't pay for and end up in debt to their eyeballs, and you have a recipe for the marital soup of death.

90210

Seven years ago when John and Valerie got married they were like most of us when we started out. Broke. Eating off a card table, driving a 1902 Gremlin, watching a TV from a garage sale, and renting that little one-bedroom apartment with the paper-thin walls. You remember, "We ain't got money, but we got love, honey, and it's a good thing too cause we ain't got no money." That is how most of us start, then we do what John and Valerie did. We go get some stuff. They replaced the Gremlin with a lease payment of $428 per month, they replaced the old TV and dad's eight track with a new entertainment center with stereo HDTV and CD player, and they replaced the card table with a cherry dining room suite. Of course the one-bedroom apartment had to go so they bought a new home in the same neighborhood as Valerie's parents. Larry Burkett says we spend the first five to seven years of our marriage trying to attain the same standard of living as our parents, only it took them thirty-five years to get there. John and Valerie had done it, they had arrived! They lived in the same area as Mom and Dad; they had a better car, nicer clothes, and definitely a better stereo system, but with all the neat new stuff came truckloads of debt. And when the bills came they started realizing that they weren't living a sitcom in Beverly Hills, and reality struck a cold hard blow. They became afraid and they were at each other's throats with a viciousness that only fear can bring. There was some serious blame throwing and selfish foxholes dug. The war was on. They came to Financial Peace University, and as they sat in the groups older couples who had weathered storms began to counsel them and lead them toward wisdom.

HEALING IS ON THE WAY

John was the first to break. He looked up one night and told Valerie, "I love you and let's just sell everything and start over, we can make it if we just stay together." Valerie honestly thought he had lost it. "Sell the salad shooter?" Aren't we all just a little stupid for stuff? Sounds corny, but John's declaration of love gave Valerie the wake-up call she needed and they began to sell some, not all, of their stuff to reduce debt. As their budget got more under control the wounds caused by the war began to heal and even the vicious twenty-something intergalactic battle came to a close with a peace accord that has now led to MORE THAN ENOUGH in their marriage and their money.

If you are under thirty and married read this chapter and the unity chapter twice and reflect not on what your spouse is doing wrong, but on what you have to change. There are several MORE THAN ENOUGH secrets and survival tips tucked in those pages.

Whether you are young or old, have been married one month or ten years, you can help your spouse through those stressful periods, when hope seems to be lost. The first thing to remember is that you are in this *together.* Don't look for whose at fault for the situation you are in, instead look for ways that you can work toward solving your problems. You will need to inspire hope in your partner. Here are a few suggestions for the ladies:

1. Remind your husband that it's not the size of his paycheck that matters, but the size of his heart.
2. Try to hold your fear in check so that you avoid nagging him.
3. Be supportive.

And for the men:

1. Don't clam up. Listen to her fears without feeling defensive; she needs to talk about them.
2. Avoid making threats—especially about leaving her.
3. Hug her.

CONTEXT IS EVERYTHING

Recently, a woman named Sally called my radio show to ask me how to start over because she had just filed bankruptcy that day. "The collectors were calling and calling, promising to sue us, it was all we could do," she said through the tears. How much debt did she file bankruptcy on? A lousy $9,000. That kind of stupidity occurs only when you lose a sense of where you are. You and I are shocked that she couldn't see a way out of only $9,000 in debt and yet really all she lost was hope.

Hope is also lost when perspective is lost. This thief of hope comes to visit when we cannot see how important an event or problem really is. After years of counseling the financially distressed I am sure that most bankruptcies, like Sally's, are filed on emotion, not as a result of a logical analysis of the situation. Most folks had other things that could be done and just lost the emotional energy to fight another day. Many people feel that spiraling bankruptcy filings are the result of Americans losing their character. Some say we have more filings today than in the 1950s be-

cause the "me" generation just won't take responsibility
for their debts. I work with these people every day and I
don't believe that. Yes, there are some spoiled brats and a
few con artists, but most filers are regular, good, hard-
working people who had something bad happen that
landed them in a mess; left with no hope, they mistakenly
filed bankruptcy.

The biggest difference in our nation's character between now and the 1950s is not with the consumer, but
with the financial industry. Back in the good ole days, few
people had one credit card, much less a dozen of them.
But today, the financial industry is after our money; over
three billion credit card offers were mailed out last year. I
have on file letters from banks and credit card companies
offering $100,000 lines of credit to numerous children un-
der the age of twelve. I also have letters offering credit to
dead people as well as several cats and dogs. Combine this
absurdity with collection tactics that make the KGB look
tame and you have a recipe for bankruptcy. The consumer
has made some errors, but the bulk of the blame lies with
the lack of character represented in our financial institutions and their decision makers. The collectors who are
more like predators feeding on the consumer cause more
bankruptcy filings than anyone else. Think I'm making
that up? VISA's own internal study of debtors showed that
the number one "last straw" that broke the camel's back
was collection tactics. Predatory collection tactics of being
called ten times a day including at work, plus your neighbor is called, your mate and children are insulted, numer-

ous messages are left on machines, rude jerks are yelling and name calling—all this can add up to you losing your understanding of what is important. Of bankruptcy filers 49 percent say collection tactics were the last straw that caused them to lose hope, so they punted.

A BEACON OF HOPE

Are you getting the picture? Hope placed on mates will bring disappointment. Hope misplaced on careers, stuff, or organizations will set us up for a letdown. Hope placed on the false security of credit cards will lead you down the road to disaster. Hope placed properly is one of the most powerful forces you will ever know, and it will allow you to be in the **MORE THAN ENOUGH** zone. Where do you find hope? I like finding symbols that remind me of hope's power, and if you have some of those reminders around it can be uplifting.

One of my favorite stories comes from *Southern Lighthouses* by Bruce Roberts and Ray Jones. It illustrates how lighthouses give direction, protection, and how that creates hope. On September 7, 1900, one of the worst natural disasters in our nation's history occurred. A hurricane of mammoth size and intensity hit Galveston Bay, Texas. There were forty thousand residents in the community; the storm's 120 mph winds and rising water killed six thousand people. That day the Bolivar Point Lighthouse manned by keeper Harry Claiborne was more than the beacon of hope it had always been. There were sixty people who ran to the lighthouse, and Harry opened his doors to them. Those sixty people climbed the circular stairs all the way to the top and were crammed in there for hours as the water rose thirty feet above the steel doors at the bottom. The winds and the water of September 7, 1900 didn't claim those sixty people who had placed their hope on something that would not fail.

These beacons have meant hope to lost sailors for centuries. We collect lighthouses around our firm and display them because they represent what we do. We give hope and direction to the financially lost. The lighthouse, or correctly placed hope, not only gives accurate direction, it also leads you to a safe harbor of MORE THAN ENOUGH. A safe harbor is where rest, repair, and the restocking of provisions occurs so that we can sail again. We can sail again with renewed hope and corrected direction. We can sail again with our wounds healed. We can sail again with the strength to help other lost sailors.

Hope correctly placed does not disappoint. Hope placed on things that fade will never fail to leave you tossed in the winds of life. Today we have to change and reevaluate where we are placing our hope. Our past is an indicator of what doesn't and does work, but is not to be dwelt on. I have heard it said, "Yesterday is history, tomorrow's a mystery, today is a gift, that's why they call it the *present.*"

The folklore of lighthouses and the image of the ray of light in the midst of a dark and stormy night are potent reminders of the power of hope. They have become a symbol in my own life and work. They may touch you as well, and if they do, make them a part of your life so that they can represent strength and hope when you need them. If they don't, take some time now to think about what such a symbol would be for you. Are there particular stories that you remember from your childhood that offer comfort and hope? Was there a lesson that a parent, teacher, or mentor taught you that might provide a symbol of hope? Find and define your symbol and bring it into your present. Perhaps you will want to post a quotation from the book from which your symbol comes in a prominent place in your home; perhaps you will find a picture that represents it. The method isn't important; what is vital is that you make it a part of your present life.

THE REAL WORLD

Life gives us some events that lend us perspective. Every so often things happen that make a real pointed statement showing us what is real and what is important. Those events, even if tragic, give us energy because our hope is made fresh when we have a clean measuring stick to use to measure other problems against.

A few weeks ago in the predawn hours Sharon and I were startled by a phone call waking us. When the phone wakes me in the dark I always think something terrible must have happened. I sat straight up and with my heart beating too fast answered the phone. Some friends were on the line and the lady had gone into labor with their second child. The baby was in trouble and this young couple was scared. I got showered and dressed and headed to the hospital, praying as I went. By the time I got there our prayers were answered and the baby had stabilized. Since we aren't *that* close I was asked to sit in the hall during delivery. For the next hour I sat reading the latest Tom Clancy novel and waiting. Suddenly there it was, that sound that can make anyone smile: that first cry of a new life coming into the world. I got to hold that brand new baby when he was less than twenty minutes old. We all understand that new life represents hope. I was still at the office by 9:00 A.M., but my day was energized. The guy who almost hit me because he ran the red light as I left the hospital didn't seem to matter as much, because I had just shared in one of those events that give you perspective and renew your hope.

My pastor shared an excellent observation with me. A mother, the instant that she knows she is with child, lives every moment in anticipation of her deliverance of hope. After a time she cannot take a step, make a move, and think a thought that is disassociated from the coming of her hope. In America, people are supposed to ignore the obvious fact that a woman is with child. In France the case is quite the contrary. If a man is introduced to a woman who is an expectant mother, it is the height of politeness for him to congratulate her. "Je vous félicite de votre espérance." "I congratulate you on your hope" is a common phrase among the cultured.

TOOLS TO CREATE HOPE

Just as a woman literally becomes pregnant with hope, we too can choose to become pregnant with the hope of new possibilities and opportunities if we keep perspective. Looking at hope-stealing events and problems across the scope of time helps you to keep that perspective. If you are struggling financially, I suggest you begin journaling, keeping a daily written account of the major problems of the day or week. When I was going broke, journaling was suggested to me. If I was having a bad day or week and the problems seemed to be something that I would never get through I would read in my journal about the problems and worries from six months before. Suddenly I could see how what I was facing was going to look minor when placed on the calendar. Now, ten years later, when I read some of the life-or-death things I thought I was facing then, they seem almost funny. Journaling will give you perspective and protect your hope.

SOUP IS GOOD FOR YOU

Another thing I suggest to folks who feel like the finances are completely beyond repair and they just can't make it another day is to serve soup. Go to your local homeless shelter and volunteer to serve soup for the lunch rush. Most folks don't know what real problems are, and the serving of soup will make you ashamed for having worried about whether there was enough in the budget to give Barky the schnauzer a haircut.

When I had lost hope one morning in the middle of our financial disaster I was reading my Bible as the sun came up and discovered this scripture: Romans 5:3–4 says, "And not only that, but we also glory in tribulations, knowing that tribulation produces perseverance; and perseverance, character; and character, hope." Problems give us the ability to hang on and that ability changes who we are. When our character is permanently molded by the trial we are stronger and the end result is hope. Hope is: The best is yet to be. I have heard it said that sorrow looks back, worry looks around, while faith looks up. Dinah Shore put it well: "There are no hopeless situations, only people who are hopeless about them."

ALONE AGAIN, NOT SO NATURALLY

Sherry, with her lips trembling, told her story one night in our group. She told of how scared she was as a twenty-five-year-old young woman trying to raise two small children after her husband deserted them two years before. Sherry told us of working two and three minimum-wage jobs just to keep the electricity on and the rent paid. Through the sobs she told us of her fears for her four-year-old son and his strong will and her daughter with no Dad in the house and Mom working all the time. Her emotion just about broke her as she cried in hopelessness, "How do I fix this mess?"

Thankfully there was a single lady in her early fifties named Amy in that group. While no one else in the group had a clue how to fix this young girl's mess Amy had the answer. The answer was, and is, hope. Amy told of being in almost exactly the same situation twenty-five years earlier. She described overwhelming fear and crying herself to sleep many nights. She was cutting hair for a living and couldn't make two frayed ends meet. What did she do? Nothing magical, she just didn't quit. She kept learning, reading, and growing. Over time, she finished her degree at night, opened her own business, and one baby step at a time moved forward, slowly becoming solid. Amy had tears flowing down her face telling Sherry that now her kids were grown and college educated, she is debt free, with rental property and mutual funds, and "It can happen to you too, Sherry." Did we fix Sherry's mess? No, but Amy gave her perspective, a new lens to look at life through. A smile of determination, not from a magic pill but determination born of hope in the future, came to Sherry before she left that night. It's like what the Swiss theologian Emil Brunner said, "What oxygen is to the lungs, such is hope to the meaning of life."

CHIN UP, SHOULDERS BACK

Is your hope running low today? I promise you if you will guard and build up these four areas your hope will become overflowing.

1. You cannot see failure as permanent, only as a building block. You have to find reality and place your hope there, not on the sinking sand of stuff, people, or institutions.
2. Find perspective by looking at events and problems in relation to time and properly placed priorities.
3. Continue to feed your vision and goals with values that are deeply rooted.
4. Use character that brings vision to lift your chin up, and as your chin raises so will your level of hope.

LIFE LESSONS AT THE BALL FIELD

Our three children play Little League ball, and after years in the ballpark I am convinced that you can learn how to live life and how not to live life by watching people. Eight-year-old girls' competitive softball is pretty intense, and the parents of course add several levels to the intensity. I remember one afternoon when the game was on the line and this little girl came up to bat. She knew how to swing, when to swing, and what kind of pitch to swing at, but when you are eight and the pressure is on sometimes nothing seems to work. When you are thirty-eight and the pressure is on sometimes nothing seems to work either. Strike one, strike two, ball one, the tears come, a pitiful swing, and the game is over. A devastated little girl walks toward her coach and the dugout with tears streaming. All sixty parents and forty kids watch as the scene unfolds.

Before she reaches the dugout she hears a familiar voice, her father's. She turns to see him with his arms out and she runs to a badly needed hug. He dries her tears, reminds her that Babe Ruth struck out more than anyone did; failure is a building block. He reminds her that it is a *game* and not to place hope in wrong things. Then this wise father lifts her chin and lets her eyes focus on the snow cone stand, and hope returns as events are put in perspective.

REAL HOPE, A REAL LIGHTHOUSE

If you listen for his voice, when you hear it you will turn and see your heavenly Father's arms open wide for a hug, and he will lift your chin just as the wise ballpark dad did. Jeremiah 29:11 says, "For I know the thoughts I think toward you, says the Lord, thoughts of peace and not of evil, to give you a future and a *hope.*" Place your hope there and you will not be disappointed.

People who have MORE THAN ENOUGH in relationships and build wealth all share the characteristic of a hope that will not be denied. They share a hope that is real and no matter what the circumstances the people who are winning are the ones who understand where to place their hope. They understand how much energy comes to you and through you when you exercise your decision to maintain hope. John Johnson, the editor of *Ebony* magazine, says, "Men and women are limited not by their intelligence, nor by their education, not by the color of their skin, but by the size of their hope."

Build the size of your hope today. Remember and put into practice these lessons:

1. Hope is an act of will; it is a decision.
2. Failure is normal; it will happen. Don't allow failure to steal your hope.
3. Hope allows you to act, rather than being stuck in the mud.
4. If you and your spouse are in the midst of a crisis, help each other to find the hope that will guide you through it.
5. Hope will not be found in things, institutions, people, or stuff.
6. Do not use credit cards or shopping sprees to make yourself feel better; these are not generators of hope but rather robbers of it.
7. Use a symbol of hope—be it a lighthouse or something else—as a way to raise your chin toward heaven when you lose direction.
8. Give to others because in giving you will find perspective and with it hope.
9. Remember your visions and goals because the road toward making them a reality offers hope.

THE STORY CONTINUES

Out of core *values, vision* is born. **Vision** is put into work clothes and becomes **goals.** Shared **goals** give you **unity** with those who are on the journey with you. **Values, vision,** and **unity** repair broken **hope** and build **hope** into the fuel that fires the rocket.

 Thoughts from Sharon . . .

One thing that we all need to remember is that we have to give hope and encouragement to one another. I'll never forget the day we filed bankruptcy. It seemed as if everything was gone. I felt like I had no hope.

The fear, loneliness, and hurt all arrived in a matter of minutes. I kept worrying what would become of us. After days of losing touch with the world, I knew that hope would be one of the key answers to our survival: hope that our family would stay together, hope that we would be able to make a living, and hope that we would not fall apart and lose it all again.

My hope was answered and yours can be too. My hope for you is that your battles will be won. Keeping everything in perspective and knowing that no one can take your hope will make this a reality instead of a dream. Remember, hope is on your side as long as you keep it there.

Keys to the More Than Enough Mansion

1. Change is very hard and we change only when the pain of *same* is greater than the pain of change.
2. Cleansing cries and hinge pins are signals that we are ready.
3. Values really do matter and real values are the foundation of everything to come.
4. Integrity—real deep integrity, even with the little things—is vital because deception destroys.
5. Connectedness is key; take time to use the sidewalks that connect you to family, friends, and coworkers.
6. Vision that is rooted in values is the only vision that will last.
7. Vision makes you a long-term investor, not living for the moment.
8. Goals are the building blocks of vision, vision in work clothes.
9. Model for and teach your children about vision and goals.
10. Opposites attract and men and women are different; identify and admit those differences and use each other's strengths for MORE THAN ENOUGH.
11. Men, build an emergency fund and leave it alone; it will change the way your wife treats you.
12. Budgeting together brings tremendous oneness

to your marriage, but you must die to selfishness; the "you" in "unity" must be silent.

13. Hope is lost when it is placed in people, stuff, and institutions.

14. Hope is lost when we believe failure is permanent and we lose perspective.

15. Hope is an act of the will and moves people to action.

16. Return to strong values and the vision born of them to rekindle your hope.

6

Accountability: How to Get an A in Conduct

Ten, nine, eight, seven, six, five, four, three, two, one, *midnight*! The confetti flies and we cheer another New Year. How many of these New Year's Eve celebrations have we attended? How many resolutions, promises to be better, vows to solve our problems have we made? We resolve to lose weight, we resolve to get out of debt, we resolve to be kinder, we resolve to add $100 to our savings account every month this year. These resolutions will never see the light of January 7. Over the last ten years, according to polls, the number one and number two resolutions we have made are to lose weight and get out of debt. Yet we live among some of the fattest debtaholics the world has ever seen. Every year Americans' waistlines get bigger as their net worths get smaller. Those resolutions are a joke! They are little more than wishes. We know life would be better without extra pounds and another credit card. Why don't we just fix it? Why don't we just say no?

Resolutions are wishes we make to ourselves. They have no teeth in them. We give our resolutions teeth when we share them with someone else who will hold us to them. The threat of shame before, or the promise of encouragement from, your accountability partner is the most powerful motivator for change known.

Our lives are like gardens. If fertilized with continued learning, watered with spiritual renewal, pruned from bad influence, and weeded of bad habits our lives will be beautiful. If left unattended, the bugs of bad influence and the weeds of bad habits will take over and ruin our lives. Clifford G. Baird says we need gardeners in our lives. The gardeners will be positive influences, hold us accountable for our behavior, and insist that we make a habit of what is good for us. Accountability and support are the tools of the gardener.

WHEN THERE ARE NO GARDENERS

Jodie and Jim had been married for five years when they came to see me for financial counseling. Jodie worked as a saleswoman for a small manufacturing company and Jim had a good job as a production supervisor at a nearby printing plant. Together they earned about $80,000 a year, a comfortable living. And yet they were facing a crisis: $25,000 worth of debt and a child on the way. They had recently moved to the Southeast from the West Coast where both of their parents still lived. Not only were they beat by their mounting debt, but they also felt isolated in their new community. As we worked through Jodie and Jim's money issues, it became clear that neither of them felt they had anyone they could rely on for advice, comfort, or accountability.

All too often we don't have gardeners in our lives. Financial problems, marital problems, career problems, spiritual challenges, and health problems will attack each of us. No one makes it through life without challenges. Some of the challenges are so big we feel we will sink under their weight. When life ties you up and throws you in a pit you have to make choices. You have to decide what to do at the bottom. When some folks get smacked so hard they can't breathe, they choose to sit and examine and talk about those scars the rest of their lives. Clifford G. Baird says, "People wallow in mediocrity knowing what they should do." We know in our minds that staying in the pit isn't smart; but it is our pit and it feels safe. Our very own pit is like sitting in a dirty diaper. We are sitting in mess and it stinks; but it is warm and it is ours, so some folks choose to stay.

PIT LADDERS

As Jodie and Jim learned, getting out of the pit is not easy and requires surrounding ourselves with people who love us enough to be mirrors we can look into to find the flaws that dug the pit in the first place. None of us likes self-examination that points out that we are the cause of our own problems. It's even worse when someone else is pointing out that we have caused, or at least contributed to, the misfortune we find ourselves in. As Norman Vincent Peale says, "The trouble with most of us is that we would rather be ruined by praise than saved by criticism."

Getting out of the pit requires we surround ourselves with people who love us enough to support us and lift us up when we are at our ugliest. When we hurt so badly and our hope is so low that we throw a huge pity party, unconditional love has to be there to wrap warmth and compassion around us so healing can begin. Accountability and support are the ladders that lift us from life's pits: accountability because it is the mirror we look into and see our character and behavior flaws; support because when we hurt we simply need help, compassion, and a hand to reach down into the pit to lift us out when our strength is gone. For Jodie and Jim, this meant reaching out to their parents whom they had been afraid to confess their problems to, making each other their primary accountability partner, and joining one of our small groups.

I HATE SMALL GROUPS

Personally I hate sitting in a small group to discuss my trash or some preselected canned topic. Sharon and I attend a lot of marriage seminars because we want to learn all we can to make our marriage excellent. They are always calling for small groups and I always want to sneak off to lunch, because I'm afraid we are going to have to talk about sex or something. Nothing wrong with sex, I'm just not into having discussions about it with people other than Sharon. Many people don't like the idea of attending a small group to support them or hold them accountable to get out of the pit. The thing is small groups work! The most powerful form of behavior modification is the properly run small group. Twelve-step groups growing out of the success of Alcoholics Anonymous have sprung up everywhere about virtually everything. When properly conducted, these groups save people's lives and can be a great ladder out of a pit.

In our Internet, cable, and voice mail culture, touching instead of "teching" people has a very powerful impact. Small groups are where real people get the chance to touch and be touched by other real people. The groups work because each person in them shares a common problem or desire to improve upon a situation. As you move through the process you can share your triumphs and own up to your defeats within a supportive community. When you need a hug, someone is there to give you one, and when you need a kick in the butt, there are plenty of volunteers!

Why are these groups so important in our society today? In part because we have lost the art of the mentor in this country. Becoming an apprentice used to be the only way to enter a trade, but now we graduate from school and have all the answers and demand huge starting salaries only to discover that experience does matter. In generations past when a young couple was married they were surrounded and counseled not only by their parents, but also by older men and women in their church and community. We have the worst divorce rate in our history, and you will find that if you attempt to give counsel to someone who didn't earnestly beg you to, he will tell you it is "none of your business." You will hear, if you are over forty, that you are "out of touch" since we have decided to worship youth rather than revere the wise gray head. We have lost the art of disciplining, mentoring, or apprenticing each other through hard times. The properly run small group returns these lost arts to your life and you will have MORE THAN ENOUGH because of it.

PERSONAL FINANCE IS MORE
PERSONAL THAN FINANCE

Personal finance is 80 percent behavior and only 20 percent head knowledge. And that is why the small group is so powerfully effective in dealing with money matters. The small group seminars we run include people who are both financially healthy and financially hurting. We hold you accountable for doing smart things like being on a spending plan and cutting up credit cards. People can survive without filing bankruptcy in an environment of support, encouragement, and hope. People can be made to look at the mistakes of overspending, debt, no plan, and no savings. They can be forced to change those behaviors and that leads folks to MORE THAN ENOUGH. And if you're already in the black financially, a small group can force you to put your good intentions into practice.

In a small group you gain a lift to work through, up, and out of the pit. Some pits are deeper than others and take longer to climb out of. Regardless of what your pit is—and maybe it is just a pothole—you can gain perspective by being within a properly run small group. The group will help you to realize that what happens *in* you is more important than what has happened *to* you. We have to take the past, learn from it, and put it behind us so what happens in us—personal growth and character change—is much more important than the pain that caused the personal growth.

LOVE AND MARRIAGE

While the small group provides a community of accountability, if you are married your primary source of accountability is your spouse, for better or for worse. Most couples don't see this as a blessing, but instead tend to protect turf and even lie to each other about money. Couples who want the level of unity we have talked about need to be willing to use each other for accountability and support. Sharon and I have made a pact that nothing major financially will be done without agreement with the other. This pact is sometimes a real pain. There are times I really want to spend some money on something and I feel like I am going into the principal's office to get permission; sometimes she feels the same way. Yet that short-term pain and giving up my "rights" has brought us closer and closer together. The trust and respect we have for each other because we don't have any "little secrets" has caused our marriage to prosper. Not only has our marriage prospered, but also we make fewer bad financial decisions and no major money decisions on impulse. Sounds a little controlling and maybe a little boring, but I assure you we love the benefits of increased intimacy and wealth.

NAGGING IS NOT GOOD, DUH

Mild amusement was on Christy's face as she was telling me in a counseling session that she just couldn't get her husband Bill to budget. The look on her face was that of a mom with a spoiled kid she thought was cute. Men need to feel useful, so that when wives "take care" of the bills and indirectly put down their husbands as if they are not competent, it can only lead to one thing: The husbands won't be involved. Who needs the insult of a snobbish look as if we are too stupid or lazy to have valid input on financial issues?

Ladies, if you are being reasonable and your husband just doesn't see the need to be involved in financial decisions, the way to cure that is to make him feel useful. Try asking for his help using statements like these that have worked for wives:

1. "Honey, I need *your help.*"
2. "Would you *invest* some time into our marriage by helping me with this?"
3. "Sweetheart, it would be such a *help to me,* if you could sit down with me so that we can figure this out together."

In addition, you can use a lesson that many marriage counselors teach: Use "I feel" statements when trying to communicate ideas in areas that can cause fights. When you say "I feel abandoned when you won't help with the bills," it is gentler than saying "you abandoned me and your children because you won't help with the bills." To soften the blows a little more you can precede "I feel" statements with a light disclaimer of "I am sure you didn't mean it this way, but . . ."

The one surefire way to drive your husband away from helping you is to nag. Nagging won't work. Men really hate nagging and it will drive a wedge in the communication between you that may take years to remove. Men, if you don't want your wives to nag, it is time to come to the plate to bat. Desperate women nag and eventually become bitter, mean women, so the nagging will become professional. Ed Cole says, "When a man refuses to act like a man his wife will act like his mother."

"CHERISH" IS THE WORD I PRESCRIBE

Men, if you are trying to get your wives to agree to a spending plan and stick to it, you need to remember a couple of things. First, control is not what I am talking about here; agreement is what we are after, so you have to be willing to back off your turf often. Ladies need to feel cherished. Cherished does not mean coddled, talked down to, or treated like a prize horse. Cherishing involves respect of strength and intellect existing side by side with love from you and your desire to care for her. Cherishing means "I'll die for you, not because you are weaker or lesser in any way, but because I love you." When wives feel cherished they love to be involved in budgets and in planning for your future. Most ladies I have counseled over the years won't talk about money because they are tired of being bullied, manipulated, or sold "his" program. One lady told me, "I'd rather deal with a cheap used-car salesman than listen to him trying to convince me to do something I know in my heart is stupid."

So if you are trying to get your wife to share in budgeting and planning, you need to treat her with respect. Try approaching her like this:

1. "Honey, I'd really like to have *your advice* on our budget."
2. "We need to think about how we are going to save money, but I can't do this *without you*."
3. "Our future is important, and *both* of us need to plan it *together*."

A SPECIAL TIME

Gentlemen, there is a special time when your wives really need you to step up and take the reins. I am not saying completely take over without input, but I am saying at this time a lady needs you to care for her by handling financial and other workloads. When your mate is carrying a child she needs and deserves your extra help. If you are struggling financially, she does not need to deal with collectors during a pregnancy. Most collectors are predatory. They will take advantage of her fatigue and hormonal swings in her body to bring out heavy emotions. She is more sensitive to security issues and has more of a tendency to fear the future and struggle with hope, and sometimes because of the chemistry and the fatigue she is just not thinking clearly. Some of you are thinking this is a totally sexist observation. I do not intend to be insulting, but it is a fact that ladies act differently when pregnant and do deserve some extra help. If that makes me sexist paint me pink and call me pig.

SINGLE IS NOT ALONE

Those who are married have built-in accountability partners. So if you are single, you should seek out a series of counselors, advisers, and friends who can support and hold you accountable. When making money decisions, you are wise if you review what you are doing with someone else. Who? First, the person should be someone who really has your best interest at heart, who loves you enough to say when something is stupid even if it hurts your feelings. Secondly, this should not be someone who is broke. People who do not have money are not people you get financial advice from. If you are in divorce court, I don't need your input on my marriage and I don't take financial advice from broke people.

Seek the counsel of your pastor, your parents, your boss, or maybe another relative, but not your shopping buddy. Develop your budget and review it with your accountability partner. Don't buy anything over $300 without discussing the purchase with this adviser and whether it is right in your situation. Remember this person must be willing and have permission from you to be brutally honest. I have had people tell me they can't seek the counsel of their parents because of a damaged relationship. If your parents are mature, balanced people, not some kind of abusers, then maybe this is a sign you need to repair the relationship. "My dad is who I should ask about money," said Mike, a twenty-four-year-old single guy in our group, one night, "but I can't because we had a fight several years ago and I promised myself I would never ask his advice." Several people in the group gently and not so gently suggested to Mike that the problem was his pride and maybe part of growing up was to make things right with his dad. Mike did meet with his dad and the relationship was not only healed over the next several months, but has blossomed as Mike reached out for help on financial decisions.

WHEN IT IS HARD TO GIVE ADVICE

A really tough set of people to hold accountable and to support are your parents. They don't want your advice or input. I call this the "powdered butt syndrome." Once someone has powdered your butt they really don't ever want your advice. You may be a brain surgeon and your dad is proud of you, but he will seek a second opinion if he has a headache. Almost every week someone calls my radio program to ask how to get Mom or Dad to save or get them to quit borrowing on credit cards. You can't force yourself on people who don't want to be held accountable, and yet you have a responsibility to your parent to step in if the stupid financial behavior is so bizarre that it must be addressed.

I remember the case of Mindy, whose mother had been widowed for just over a year when she began going on trips to Las Vegas with a local seniors group. At first, Mindy was pleased: "Mom was finally getting out and not sitting at home in misery." But then Mindy's mother began asking her daughter for money; she didn't admit it but she was losing a great deal while gambling. She lost so much money that she was putting her future in jeopardy. I counseled Mindy to take the same approach as she would if Mom had an alcohol problem. Mindy called a family meeting at which loving brothers, sisters, and other close family members gathered to explain in person to Mom how afraid they were for her and how she must change. Where an addiction is involved counselors call this an intervention and that is about the only way to start the process of breaking someone away from stupid behavior.

Another way to influence Mom or Dad is to find someone who has credibility with them to explain the need to change. A brother, sister, uncle, good boss, coworker, or pastor Mom or Dad trusts will have much better luck with a wake-up call than you will. Outside experts can also be a way to wake someone up. Many times books or tapes have been used to say the same thing you were saying, but because an "author" or "financial expert" gave the same advice it is suddenly heard.

WHAT TO DO ON THE MOUNTAIN

Just because you aren't in financial or personal difficulty doesn't mean you don't need accountability partners. When times are good and you are on a mountaintop in your life you need to maximize your life and your wealth. Who you surround yourself with will determine the height you are able to climb. Your relationships and alliances are vital to having MORE THAN ENOUGH. You must fly with eagles, not scratch with turkeys. How can the synergy of turkeys create anything but getting your goose cooked? We tend to take on the characteristics, mannerisms, and eventually even the values of the people we spend time with. When you move to a new area of the country you will eventually even talk like those folks. We become desensitized to negatives around us. If you move next to a railroad track, the first couple of 3 A.M. trains will cause you to bounce off the ceiling. But after a week you will sleep right through the noise. People who live next to industrial plants that stink don't smell them anymore. The same is true of bad, unproductive, or offensive habits. We don't notice because everyone else isn't noticing. J. Oswald Sanders says, "If a thousand people say something foolish, it's still foolish. Truth is never dependent upon consensus of opinion." Consensus of behavior by those around you will influence you by changing your behavior to match, so surround yourself with eagles. Find people who are being who you want to be and spend time with them. Your habits and values will be better because you will become like those you are hanging around with.

The synergy of eagles is incredible. When two or more are reaching for excellence together, a wonderful power is created. Few people have **MORE THAN ENOUGH** without the power of synergy. The writer and motivational speaker Zig Ziglar relates what happens when Belgian horses work together. One horse can pull 8,000 pounds. Hook two together and they immediately pull over 18,000 pounds, more than double. With one week's training the same team can pull over 25,000 pounds, more than triple. The power of being connected to people pulling the same way adds insight, ingenuity, ideas, values, energy, and good habits that can mushroom. One plus one no longer equals two. As Proverbs 24:6 says, ". . . And in a multitude of counsellors there is safety."

GROUPS THAT MEET ON THE MOUNTAIN

Napoleon Hill, in the classic *Think and Grow Rich*, says that we should form Mastermind groups of people who can synergize with us and influence us to become even bigger than our dreams. Dan Miller, one of the leading career coaches in the nation and a personal friend, forms groups that he calls Eagle Alliances. Dan gathers people with a common interest and each member then has accountability and support and, more important, peers with which they can brainstorm. He says a group of business people can have many creative ideas and solutions to problems for each other. The possible common bond can be anything. Most cities have inventors' groups where you can learn about patenting your invention. I was an officer in a real estate investors group, which does a wonderful job trading ideas, teaching, even swapping leads for contractors and deals. You might want to call your group Eagle Alliances or, if you have a sense of humor, Turkey Busters.

If things are going well in your life, take that positive momentum and kick it up another notch by formally and informally forming groups of eagles around you. In your business life, your spiritual life, your relationships, and your finances you need to think about who you have surrounded yourself with and understand you will become the sum of your peers and what you read.

WHAT TO DO ALL THE TIME

On the mountains, surround yourself with eagles to maximize your wealth and your happiness in work, family, and marriage. In the valleys surround yourself with experienced folks for a hand out of the pit. On a constant basis, all the time, there is another type of permanent accountability and support. The permanence in this area comes from the very inner circle of your relationships. Your mate, your parents, other immediate family, and those few friends who are there for life make up your permanent inner circle. Those people who you are with for life are the ones who naturally lend themselves to holding you accountable and are the ones who will support you. These people will always tell you the truth, even if it hurts. They are the ones who will say when something is really stupid—and sometimes even enjoy it a little too much. These are the people who have seen us in our underwear, for whom you can't put on a mask good enough to fake it. They know when something is right and when something is wrong. While our inner circle may be bothersome, those who have MORE THAN ENOUGH learn from and receive from their inner circle.

Lifelong friends, pastors, church members, bosses, and coworkers can also serve as guides as we travel through life. They tend not to be quite as brutal with the truth as our inner circle of family members. Sometimes they may be timid about pointing out a wrong turn, but these people still fall in our inner circle and are still very important in offering us guidance and support. You should have five people whose wisdom, intent, experience, and love you trust.

I have also identified several "specialists" within my inner circle. A specialist is someone I trust beyond life for advice on one or two subject areas but I would not seek their advice or input in another area. For instance, I have one close friend from whom I can get great input on behavior, character, parenting, or marriage, but I wouldn't think of asking for financial advice from that person. If you include specialists in your list, it will probably grow to around ten people.

You definitely need a confidant and adviser in spiritual matters who you can have access to so you can continue to grow in that area as well. My pastor and several elders in my church are who I seek counsel from on matters like perception, vision, integrity, God's leading.

Take a few minutes now and list the members of your inner circle below:

1. _____
2. _____
3. _____
4. _____
5. _____

If you can only name two or less then you should begin to develop some more quality relationships outside your family. If you have a seriously dysfunctional family, you will want to spend more time developing your other areas of counsel. Or perhaps there are relationships within your family that need healing; you need to spend some time cultivating that part of your garden so that you can add those members of your family to your inner circle.

Now think about who you could add to your inner circle as specialists. List below the names and areas of expertise you would go to each person for:

1. _____ who is an expert in _____ .
2. _____ who is an expert in _____ .
3. _____ who is an expert in _____ .
4. _____ who is an expert in _____ .
5. _____ who is an expert in _____ .

Do your experts cover the spectrum of your life? Have you thought of people who can help you with finances, career strategy, relationships, family issues, and spiritual questions?

As you think about who the members of your inner circle are and who else you might need to add, remember that the people on your inner circle list need to be people who can keep their mouths shut. I have known authority figures and "good friends" who have become the source of rumors and gossip; they forgot that they had been asked for counsel, not to be a source for *The National Enquirer*! Be careful who you allow in your inner circle.

You should also know that this process of accountability and support is not perfect: There are people involved in the process. People sometimes give well-intentioned, enthusiastic, bad advice because people are not perfect. Remember just because you take some risks when getting input doesn't mean it isn't worth it. It is worth it: Two heads are always better than one.

REAL LOVE

Years ago, I could be really mean to Sharon when I was angry. One day, a close friend overheard me on the phone being a jerk to her; later he came to my office after I had calmed down. It took a lot of courage for him to admit he hadn't always treated his mate as he should, and it took even more courage for him to tell me I needed to learn to control my anger. I didn't like this conversation mainly because I knew he was right, but that guy being strong enough to come in and tell me I wasn't acting right may have saved my marriage.

If you are in someone's inner circle, please support and hold them accountable. Holding someone else to good intent, good behavior, and wise decisions is hard. It is hard because it takes courage to discuss uncomfortable topics with others. A good way to lead into a conversation about something stupid that someone is doing is, like my friend, to first admit having done something dumber at one point. This keeps your friend, mate, or relative from thinking you are coming to preach, but lets them know your heart is humble and makes it easier for them to hear something painful. You will also need to have a relationship that can support your taking a bold stand; my friend could not have confronted me about my being a jerk to Sharon if we had not had a long and deep relationship to start with. If you try to confront someone you don't have permission from or a deep enough relationship with, you will not do any good because they won't hear you. The depth and commitment of your relationship must match or be deeper than the seriousness of the problem being confronted. Generally, to maximize the benefits of these inner-circle relationships takes a lot of time: You need to build trust, know each other's strengths and weaknesses, learn to be comfortable asking and receiving help from each other, and find effective ways to teach and learn from each other.

RESPECT OR EXPECT

When you are in a relationship that implies or expects accountability and you are too wimpy to gently confront stupid behavior, that person will lose respect for you. A pastor who won't confront adultery, a boss who won't confront laziness, or parents who won't discipline are all people we don't respect. A group leader who allows someone in the group to live in a fantasy or allows them to continue without being confronted about stupid behavior is someone the group loses respect for. People do not respect those who will not hold them accountable when they are stupid or arrogant. People do not respect those who do not have the strength to be compassionate and support them when they are hurting. Clifford G. Baird says, "When respect leaves expect comes." When you no longer respect your parent or boss "gimme" sets in. Gimme this and gimme that. A parent who does not support and hold a child accountable creates a spoiled child. Children who receive an allowance for doing nothing lose respect and come to merely expect from their parents. A husband who does not support his wife's goals and achievements nor holds her accountable to their budget creates a wife who is bitter and feels justified in spending whatever money she wants.

THERE IS A PERFECT PLACE

There is one perfect place to receive accountability and support. The wisdom is unending and the compassion is deeper than a cool mountain lake. A close relationship with your Creator, God, is an essential part of growing as a human. Many folks lead productive lives that have the feeling of being normal without that relationship. But if you have a relationship with God it brings more joy, peace, and wisdom than you can otherwise get. This relationship is the ultimate accountability and support system. A scolding during your prayer time will change your behavior more than your mom ever could. Support and healing during a conversation with your maker is the best salve known.

EVEN THE LONE RANGER HAD TONTO

The four types of accountability and support we have talked about are your paths to MORE THAN ENOUGH: small groups to make your valleys not so deep, Eagle Alliances to make your mountaintops higher, family and friends to be with you and guide you through thick and thin, and a relationship with God to provide the ultimate support and accountability system. We can't be effective and enjoy the benefits of wealth and healthy relationships by ourselves. To reach another notch of peace, excellence, and wealth you need to make sure that you have your own accountability system in place and that you are supporting others in your life as well. What do you need to do to get an A in accountability?

For myself:

1. Who is my main accountability partner?
2. Am I spending time with the right people?
3. Do I need to change my calendar so that there is room for a prayer group, a class, or a meeting to brainstorm?
4. Do I have a budget, savings, and investing plan in place that I have shared with others who will hold me accountable?
5. Do I need to find specialists to add to my inner circle?
6. Do I need to spend time to deepen my relationships with the people who are or should be in my inner circle?
7. Do I need to strengthen my relationship with God?

For others:

1. Have I reached out to those in my family who need me?
2. Do I have some kind of expertise that I should be offering to others?
3. Am I supporting my spouse so that we can reach our goals together?
4. Is there someone close to me who is going down the wrong path who I should help?

Accountability and support brought into your life on purpose helps you to review and adjust your values, which activates a renewed vision and goals. Having loving friends and family brings unity and powers up your hope. Offering aid and comfort to your spouse, children, parents, and friends gives them hope. Having your hope based on truth will raise it yet another notch, giving you the ability to walk in true joy. You will simply build more wealth because you don't make the same mistakes over and over or make as many new mistakes when you seek wise counsel. You will recover from valley or pit experiences faster and with more hope having loving guides in your life. The people who have More Than Enough are people who have learned the value of accountability and support—both as providers and receivers.

THE STORY CONTINUES

Out of core *values, vision* is born. *Vision* is put into work clothes and becomes *goals.* Shared *goals* give you *unity* with those who are on the journey with you. *Values, vision,* and *unity* repair broken *hope* and build *hope* into the fuel that fires the rocket. The rocket is kept between the ditches by *accountability* and *support.*

Thoughts from Sharon . . .

Being a mom and housewife, I sometimes feel like I need lots of accountability partners. I have different groups for accountability that I depend on a lot.

My first accountability partner is, of course, my spouse. Dave and I talk about everything and we never make a major decision without discussing it first.

Church partners are also a big help. Once a month a small group of women from our church meet for lunch and prayer. We have a great time fellowshipping with one another, but we feel we can be open with each other and ask for special prayer requests when needed.

Another place I sometimes turn to is school. The schools our children attend have a special bond between parents and children. I feel as if I could go to any Mom there and ask for guidance and I would receive it with open arms.

We have also found couples accountability groups play an important role in our marriage. You have read many times when Dave has mentioned all the marriage seminars we have attended. Well, we really have and they do work. We believe that you must surround yourselves with couples who believe and think as you do. We have belonged to several supper clubs within our church and have made some close friends through these. There are times when we really depended on these couples.

And last, but not least, is being accountable to God each and every day. The bottom line is truth, honesty, openness, and development of close relationships that hold us all accountable to each other.

Keys to the More Than Enough Mansion

1. Change is very hard and we change only when the pain of *same* is greater than the pain of change.
2. Cleansing cries and hinge pins are signals that we are ready.
3. Values really do matter and real values are the foundation of everything to come.
4. Integrity—real deep integrity, even with the little things—is vital because deception destroys.
5. Connectedness is key; take time to use the sidewalks that connect you to family, friends, and coworkers.
6. Vision that is rooted in values is the only vision that will last.
7. Vision makes you a long-term investor, not living for the moment.
8. Goals are the building blocks of vision, vision in work clothes.
9. Model for and teach your children about vision and goals.
10. Opposites attract and men and women are different; identify and admit those differences and use each other's strengths for MORE THAN ENOUGH.
11. Men, build an emergency fund and leave it alone; it will change the way your wife treats you.
12. Budgeting together brings tremendous oneness

to your marriage, but you must die to selfishness; the "you" in "unity" must be silent.

13. Hope is lost when it is placed in people, stuff, and institutions.

14. Hope is lost when we believe failure is permanent and we lose perspective.

15. Hope is an act of the will and moves people to action.

16. Return to strong values and the vision born of them to rekindle your hope.

17. Small groups for support and encouragement are the most powerful form of behavior modification known.

18. When holding your spouse accountable use "I feel" statements that aren't so threatening.

19. Pride busting and encouragement when needed are the lost art of the mentor.

7

Intensity: Feeling the Fervor

When Rob and his wife, Joline, came to see me they were at the end of their rope. They had spent the last decade working part-time jobs trying to reduce their debt and create wealth, but they didn't have a plan. Finally, Rob looked at their debt and said, "This has got to go." He and Joline put a spending, debt reduction, and savings plan into practice. What did this mean for them? Over the next eighteen months, Rob worked, incredibly, four jobs. During that time, Joline had the responsibility for their two kids, the house, making sure they stayed on their budget—a lot of it without Rob's presence and input. But the way Rob and Joline figured it, so what if he missed dance recitals, ball games, and teacher conferences for eighteen months; so what if Joline had to fend for herself and her family without Rob for eighteen months? Their goal was to never miss another of their children's events, never to have to worry about another collector at the door, never to have to go it alone again, never to have to scrimp to find extra dollars to save for their future.

By the end of eighteen months, Rob and Joline managed to erase $85,000 of debt, get their savings and investments up to $50,000, and look forward to being able to keep adding $500 a month to their investments. During that time, Rob also had an idea that would save his employer thousands of dollars. When the idea was implemented, it changed the process of production at his manufacturing plant and saved several steps on the assembly line. As a reward for his idea, Rob was given a $4,000 bonus. The method that allowed Rob and Joline to achieve these extraordinary feats is intensity.

This story amazes us because Rob and Joline seem so unusual in today's society. Where has all the passion gone? Why do we not get fired up anymore about anything except sports? Have we become so "civilized" that we don't care enough to feel intensity about anything? People seem to be walking around with vacancy signs in their eyes: "Nobody's home." Hey, with some folks it looks like there isn't even anyone coming up the driveway.

Intensity is a key ingredient in the lives of people who win. Those with intensity win the battle to get MORE THAN ENOUGH. They have prosperous relationships and they build wealth because they will stand for no less. Intensity is birthed in your values that cause you to care about something. That desire for something or someone bigger than yourself gives you vision, which leads to the fire of hope. Intensity can't help but erupt when you incorporate into your life the proven keys we have discussed up to this point: values, vision, unity, hope, and accountability. If you haven't put those lessons into practice, go back and read any and all of the chapters you don't yet have a real handle on. Why? Because intensity increases and strengthens as more and more of your life flows from these habits.

THE WINDS OF CHANGE ARE BLOWING

Intensity is also a decision. Intensity is a decision to attack, to have passion, and to purposefully put power into your thoughts and actions. Sister Kenny said, "It is better to be a lion for a day than a sheep all your life." You have to go and kill something. You have to have goals flowing from your values and vision. You have to have the strength and the energy to run through roadblocks and never look back until you reach your goals. "The key to life is accepting challenges. Once someone stops doing this, he's dead" is the way Bette Davis summed it up. Intensity has changed many a mediocre man or woman into a warrior for the cause of MORE THAN ENOUGH. They won't be denied. Do you hear the theme to *Rocky* playing? I think I do.

If you don't like where you are, you have to change what you have been doing. And that takes intensity. But the fact is most people aren't intense enough. Intensity makes you bold, it makes you walk a little faster, and it scares some people. I've heard it said that if you want something you've never had you'll have to do something you've never done. Wandering around being normal doesn't cut it for those of us who will not settle for less than MORE THAN ENOUGH. Andrew Carnegie, one of the wealthiest men ever, said it best: "The average person puts only 25 percent of his energy and ability into his work. The world takes off its hat to those who put in more than 50 percent of their capacity, and will stand on its head for those few and far between souls who devote 100 percent."

FOCUS FOR FERVOR

"What is the first requirement of success?" Thomas Edison was asked. His answer? It is "the ability to apply your physical and mental energies to one problem incessantly without growing weary. If you get up at 7 A.M. and go to bed at 11 P.M., you have put in sixteen good hours, and it is certain with most men that they have been doing something all the time. The only trouble is that they do it about a great many things, and I do it about one. If they took the time in question and applied it in one direction, to one object, they would succeed." What he is saying is that intensity brings you focus; focus and singleness of purpose are the common denominators that successful people share. Light dispersed simply lights the room, but when finely focused light forms a laser that will cut steel. Focus has the power to create permanent change where nothing else will or can. You can focus. You can endure anything for a short period of time. Six months, a year, or even eighteen months—as in the case of Rob and Joline—compared with the rest of your life is a very short period of time. For that period of time you can endure virtually anything.

Do you have goals that you haven't been achieving because of a lack of focus? Most of us do and keep putting them off because we have so many things that have to be done right now. But putting off your goals only means that you lose the chance to create the things you really want while trudging through the chores of daily life. Make a list now of some of the things you've been putting off because you don't have time to focus on them. Think about every area of your life as you make your list:

Personal:

1. _____
2. _____

Financial:

1. _____
2. _____

Practical:

1. _____
2. _____

Career:

1. _____
2. _____

You may not have goals in every area, but use this time to think about what you are missing out on because you keep putting off the things you really want. As you read through the rest of the chapter, think about how you might achieve at least one of your goals in a short period of time.

"MAD" IS NOT THE WORD FOR IT

Without exception every person I have watched get out of debt quickly—and by quickly I mean in less than two years—got mad. They got so mad at their situation that they attacked. They ate, drank, and slept debt elimination. They focused. As Les Brown, the great motivator, says, "People change their lives when they say 'I've had it!' " I have seen folks pay off fifty, sixty, seventy thousand dollars and more in debt in less than a year. What did they have? Intensity.

Proverbs gives us a hint as to why this intensity works. Proverbs 6:5 gives this instruction to someone who wants to get rid of his debt: "Deliver yourself, like a gazelle from the hand of the hunter, and like a bird from the hand of the fowler." For years when I read this Proverb I would think, "Oh, well, isn't that a nice little word picture." That nice little word picture took on a whole new meaning one night when I landed on the Discovery channel while surfing channels. It was one of those animal shows and I tuned in just as a cheetah is sneaking up on a herd of gazelles. The gazelles are out there just gazelling around on the tundra apparently unaware something is getting ready to make them into lunch. The cheetah crawls through the brush closer and closer. Suddenly one of the gazelle's cheetah detector goes off and all those little gazelles get *real* attentive. Mr. Cheetah, realizing he has been detected, gives up the hiding thing and the chase is on. The cheetah, the fastest animal on land, is after his lunch. Gazelles scatter, no doubt yelling "CHEETAH!" Since the cheetah can't chase them all down, he picks a single gazelle to pursue. Now, the gazelle knows he can't outrun the cheetah, so he attempts to out-maneuver him instead. Gazelle belly about three inches off the tundra, he runs literally for his life, bobbing and weaving, cutting and darting in a manner that would make any NFL running back envious. The cheetah finally tires and the gazelle escapes. Whew! The announcer informs us that the cheetah is successful in only one out of nineteen chases.

GAZELLE INTENSITY

It occurred to me that the reason people were getting out of debt when they got mad, focused, and intense was that they were delivering themselves like a gazelle from the hand of the hunter. In fact I've coined the phrase "gazelle intensity," and when I see one of our class members who is mad at debt, I say that they are "gazelle intense." When someone is gazelle intense they do what it takes no matter what. If they are trying to get out of debt they sell so much stuff the kids are afraid they are next. If someone is gazelle intense about getting a college fund for their child he works a second job, whether it's delivering pizza or cleaning motel rooms on the weekends, until the fund is full. If someone is gazelle intense about making his marriage better he turns off the TV and starts going on date nights with his mate, and nothing bumps that off the calendar. Gazelle intensity creates motion; it takes energy and speed to the edge because nothing else matters.

That kind of intensity will always cause you to win or at a minimum have some serious fun in the game. The thing to remember is that gazelle intensity isn't just for periods of crisis, but a method through which you can achieve any result you desire.

Take the case of Alex and Sandra, two young professionals who were making over $90,000 per year and had two small children under the age of six. They had over $100,000 in credit card debt, student loans, car loans, and a boat loan. They had the money to make the monthly payments, so they didn't have creditors at their door and felt they could manage their lives on their incomes. But Alex and Sandra had a dream: to be able to live on Alex's salary while Sandra stayed home to be a full-time mom. In nine months they were debt free except for their home. How did they pay off

$100,000 in nine months? Gazelle intensity! They sold the boat and both cars, had three garage sales, sold items through the classifieds, and got on a lifestyle slash-and-burn budget. After nine months Alex called me to share his joy: "Dave, Sandra just mailed the last VISA check off and gave her two-week notice." Then he added. "We are driving two $4,000 paid-for cars and with only the mortgage to pay off we can easily live on my $55,000 income while Sandra lives her dream of being a full-time mom." When intensity comes, lives are changed, and I can promise you Alex and Sandra are much happier now.

You can do that too. I know your income may not be that large, but no matter what your goals or the roadblocks in the way, you can achieve your dreams. If you are single achieving intensity is even easier than for married couples. Sometimes couples aren't intense at the same time, which means that one of you is trying to drive a speedboat, while the other has left the anchor in the water—you don't get anywhere fast. Singles, however, when they get gazelle intensity are 100 percent into it; no one else has to be onboard and this gives the single an advantage. If you are a single parent, you may feel that you have no opportunities to use gazelle intensity to your advantage. Wrong. It may be harder for you since you have sole responsibility for your children, but I can guarantee that if you apply intensity you will find a way to increase your productivity without losing your relationship with your children. Perhaps you need to arrange for a friend to stay with your kids an evening a week while you take on that second job that will allow all of you to have enough extra cash to invest in all your futures. If you are a widow or a widower, you may feel you no longer have the energy or the desire to achieve your goals. Please don't cheat yourself! Go back to the last chapter and think again about who your accountability partner is and use your partner to help you get motivated to reach for your dreams with gazelle intensity.

SPAN, NOT SPAM

Whatever your situation, focus and intensity increase your attention span. Remember being a kid who couldn't sit still? Or better yet, let me share the story of when I was seven playing Little League baseball. I was in the second grade and my Little League team was coached by Coach Brewer, a nice, gentle man. Back then, when the dinosaurs roamed the earth, we used the same baseball as the pros, the hard one. One day, I was in center field watching, not our practice, but an airplane going overhead at thirty thousand feet. Not realizing my head was literally in the clouds, Coach Brewer hit a pop fly to center field. I never saw it. It hit me on my upper lip just below the nose and knocked me out cold. I woke up in the dugout with a coach who thought he had killed one of his players and a badly swollen lip with a strange print of a baseball's stitching on it. That's what can happen when you don't pay attention. In life, as in baseball, not keeping your head in the game can get you hurt.

"Concentration: put all your eggs in one basket and watch that basket," said Dale Carnegie. The more mature you are the longer you can maintain focus or intensity because you have a longer attention span. But if you find yourself unable to focus and concentrate on the goals you want to accomplish, you need to force yourself to be single-minded, at least for a period of time. Many of us need daily reminders to keep our focus and our intensity level up so that our attention is focused on the game at hand. Use you accountability partner to help you; ask him to nudge you along or demand that he give you a kick in the behind if you fall behind. Write down your plan of action and stick to it!

You also need to teach your children intensity, focus, and the resulting attention span; this will give them the skills for having **MORE THAN ENOUGH**. Intensity and focus are most powerful when held for long periods of time. One hour of intensity will not bring the same results as intensity for a goal held over one year. It takes practice to develop the maturity to stay focused and intense over a longer period, and you have to teach that to children. Start by having some short and reachable goals for the three- to nine-year-old crowd. You might work with them on a project such as yard work and tell them if they stay with it for the two hours needed you will all go for ice cream. Two hours is an eternity to a little guy, but it lengthens his ability to focus and stay with a goal until complete. Also ask them to create specific savings goals. Perhaps your daughter wants a new doll; help her focus on how to save the money to buy it for herself. This will allow them to develop into being savers.

As they reach a goal and you can tell they have kept the goal in their sights the entire time frame, raise the bar. Lengthen the time frame during which they save. As you do this throughout their lives it will enable them to develop the intensity and financial attention span to see years into the future. By the time they reach their early teens they should be able to have clear vision about their college years and even into retirement. We all have met forty-eight-year-olds who can't see past Friday; they have just never flexed their intensity and focus muscles so they became flabby.

THE MOTHER OF MORE: MOMENTUM

One of my favorite parts of intensity is the momentum it creates. Some folks have their feet planted firmly on the ground and move like it. Other folks understand or at least have a glimpse of the power of momentum. I used to work for a guy who said, "Even a blind hog will find an acorn to eat if he wanders enough." Another guy, at one of my many jobs, told me to "look confused, but stumble forward." Momentum is so important that it does not have to be pretty. I am constantly telling our marketing team that huge amounts of activity will beat the smart guy every time. In marketing if you create a huge splash of contacts and exposure even if it isn't perfect or well analyzed, that will create momentum where making two perfect calls will probably sell nothing. Too many times when any of us are trying to create momentum in our lives we want to do a couple of things perfectly instead of an immense level of activity that might not be as pretty, but gets that ball rolling because of the shear energy involved. Momentum is seldom created by pretty activity, but instead by tons of activity, hard work, and usually some ugly mistakes.

Momentum is strange. Whether it is in relationships, business, or finance it seems to have the same properties. It is hard to get the ball rolling. Creating momentum is as if you really are trying to get a large heavy ball to roll. It takes an immense amount of power, effort, fervor, intensity, focus, and attention span to even get the thing to budge. If you don't lower the intensity as soon as it moves, like so many do, you can continue to build its speed. We all know that once the thing starts moving it takes on a life of its own. That is why people don't get out of debt slowly and steadily; they push and go crazy for a short period of time and then they are set to build wealth the rest of their lives.

Momentum works the same way in investing. It takes twenty years of saving $325 per month at 12 percent to get the first $300,000, but the second $300,000 will be added to your account in just the next five years. Then almost another $300,000 will be there in just over three more years.

Number of Years It Took	Amount Saved
20	$321,000
25	$610,000
28	$887,000

Momentum is powerful! The intensity that creates momentum is not optional if you want build wealth.

THERE ISN'T A TOOTSIE POP
AT THE CENTER

Momentum is almost magical in its qualities. Those with momentum always look better than they are and those without it always look worse than they are. One person said, "One outstanding success can often cover a multitude of blunders." Momentum, while it does require intensity, is not hasty. At its core it has a patience born of strength and requires patience from you. A get-rich-quick mentality has at its core a laziness, a something-for-nothing thought pattern, and momentum will have nothing to do with you while you try to "get rich quick."

Some of you are like Rick who came to me for counseling several years ago. Operating a small business, Rick had the idea that everyone was out to get him; all his "luck" was bad luck and all his mean ole competitor's "luck" was good luck. After weeks of working with him he finally closed his business and gave up. He refused to accept responsibility for not having enough intensity to create momentum so his so-called luck would change. To me, Rick is a case of someone who wouldn't work hard enough and with enough intensity to get the ball rolling. He is like a lot of people I meet, people who break my heart because they have been taught to be mediocre by making a habit of moving at half speed, and they are very bitter about it. The mean ole company, my nagging spouse, my disrespectful kids, and life in general has turned on me is the attitude they have adopted. Backward momentum is as powerful and hard to stop as forward momentum. That is why the rich get richer and the poor get poorer. It is like two cars going in opposite directions on a highway at 55 mph each. They are traveling apart at 110 mph. If you are going the wrong way it takes as much energy and intensity to stop as it does to get going again in the right direction.

Are you stuck in one place and unable to move forward? Do you feel that life is "against" you, that your "luck" is bad, that someone is standing in your way? Stop and think about what's really going on. Go back and examine the goals you wrote down earlier in this chapter and pick just one of them and do something about it. Decide in your heart that you are going to change this one thing and do it. Come up with a plan and get your momentum going. Once you do you'll be able to attack every single item on your list.

IT KEEPS GOING AND GOING AND GOING

Momentum born of intensity is so powerful it can carry over generations. If character is at the core, wealth passed through generations can become a dynasty. A dynasty that gives, grows, and helps occurs when wealth is passed generationally along with values. Remember Rob and Joline at the beginning of the chapter who paid off $85,000 in debt and got their savings up to $50,000? They have generational momentum because they are planning their savings and investments for today *and* tomorrow.

Momentum like that changes family trees. And in the future their intensity can pay off, making them into today's Vanderbilts, Carnegies, and Rockefellers. You can change your family tree by setting in place these keys to MORE THAN ENOUGH, then douse them in the gasoline of intensity and let us all watch the explosion.

FORGET THE LIGHTS AND CAMERA, GIVE ME THE ACTION

Intensity also can't help but create initiative. Intensity that will not be denied is the mother of initiative. Initiative that moves you outside the rules and makes you creative comes only if you care enough to have intensity. Take the example of Louise. She had been the manager of her local bookstore for three years when a new and bigger store opened up three blocks away. Sales began to drop, and within three months they were off by 15 percent. But Louise was convinced that the store had something special to offer the community. So she asked her staff to join her on a retreat to try to find ways to turn the situation around. It wasn't easy, but they came up with several ideas to improve their service: a table in the front of the store with staff recommendations; a store-sponsored reading group, which they asked an English professor at a local college to lead; and a monthly mailing to their regular customers highlighting new books of special interest. As they put these changes into effect, Louise realized that she needed to get the word out about their improved service, so she wrote an article about why a bookstore can be at the center of the life of the community and what she and her staff were doing to make that a reality. With the down-home feel making the store a "comfortable" and approachable place to gather versus corporate plastic programs the store could flourish. Louise's intensity brought awareness of the best parts of the community bookstore to her area. Within weeks, traffic increased and sales improved even beyond the goal that she had set for the store. Louise cared enough to make sure that the new competition didn't hurt their business and in the process also created a better place for all of them.

PASS IT ON

One of the most important gifts you can teach your children is the power of initiative. Move on it! Go get it! These are lessons that need to be taught at an early age. One of the easiest ways to encourage children's initiative is to pick up on what they love to do. Is your child wild about horses? Why not take them to the local barn and have your child negotiate horseback riding lessons in exchange for mucking out stalls once a week. Is your ten-year-old a budding entrepreneur? Encourage and guide him as he sets up his first business—whether it's a lemonade stand by a local tourist trap or a lawn mowing service, he will learn how to run a business. Does your sixteen-year-old desperately want to go to Europe for the summer? Help her to think about how she could achieve this dream; take her to the library to look up what kinds of summer programs she might be interested in; ask her to come up with a savings plan that will allow her to finance at least a portion of the cost of the trip.

These lessons will teach your children that having passions means acting on them, and they will learn the skills they need to make their passions a reality. Your teen and college-ager who possess these characteristics will have real experience to bring to their job searches, making them more marketable, and they will bring passion for life to their relationships, allowing them to enjoy them more fully.

I LOVE IT WHEN A PLAN COMES TOGETHER

In our age of the Internet, databases, and surveys we have more information at our fingertips than we can possibly digest. That information is worthless without someone with the courage and initiative to do something with all of it. Dennis Rainey says, "Our culture worships information, but information without application is an empty deity." The information in this book and this chapter are no different. If you read all this information that will change your life and you do nothing, what good is it? Are you going to raise your level of intensity and passion and go for it without embarrassment? Lift your chin and grab hold for a ride on the momentum express. Yes, you will make mistakes, but as one guy said, "Those who have never made a mistake usually work for those who have." Yes, you will have to pay a price, but President Andrew Jackson, who was known for being rather intense, said, "You must pay the price if you want to secure the blessing." If you do not pay the price of intensity, momentum, attention span, and initiative you will pay the price of mediocrity. You will just be normal, and who in their heart of hearts really wants to just be normal?

Go back and look at the list of goals you made on page 161. Pick one from each category and think about how you could use intensity to make it a reality. For each goal of each category, write down one way in which you can turn your desire into a plan that uses gazelle intensity. Focus on the feeling here—the fervor, the intensity, and the focus you need to make your goal a reality.

Personal:

_____

_____

Financial:

_____

_____

Practical:

_____

_____

Career:

_____

_____

Share these thoughts with your accountability partner.
Discuss with them how these goals and your plans to create momentum and intensity fit in with your values, vision, goals. Ask them to make you accountable for them
and to help you when you find yourself slipping back into

mediocrity and negativity. But most of all, put your plans into action and enjoy the power of momentum!

The progression, the staircase, leading to the best possible marriage, the most fulfilling career, the healthiest spiritual condition, and some serious piles of money continues. Can you see it? Can you see how your values lead to the creation of your vision? Then your vision puts on street clothes in the form of goals. Unity aligns you with those you love so they can take this ride with you. Hope is the fuel that when ignited turns you, the rocket, lose with intensity, and all the while accountability is your guidance system that will keep you between the ditches. You can have **MORE THAN ENOUGH**!

THE STORY CONTINUES

Out of core *values, vision* is born. *Vision* is put into work clothes and becomes *goals.* Shared *goals* give you *unity* with those who are on the journey with you. *Values, vision,* and *unity* repair broken *hope* and build *hope* into the fuel that fires the rocket of *intensity.* The rocket of *intensity* is kept between the ditches by *accountability* and *support.*

Thoughts from Sharon . . .

Being a mother of three children and having an entrepreneur as a husband, intensity at our house can sometimes be overwhelming. Since the children were young we have tried to instill in them to always do their best. I tell them if they are going to do something, do it right the first time and they won't have to go back and correct their mistakes. It works most of the time.

Some people want to give up and take the easy way out and then complain about never having anything. We have learned over the years that it's not always going to be easy, it takes hard work and commitment, but the effort you put into something is what you will get out of it. You don't have to settle for second best, if you use your abilities to create the intensity and make a plan. You do what you have to do, and you'll be amazed at what can happen.

Keys to the More Than Enough Mansion

1. Change is very hard and we change only when the pain of *same* is greater than the pain of change.
2. Cleansing cries and hinge pins are signals that we are ready.
3. Values really do matter and real values are the foundation of everything to come.
4. Integrity—real deep integrity, even with the little things—is vital because deception destroys.
5. Connectedness is key; take time to use the sidewalks that connect you to family, friends, and coworkers.
6. Vision that is rooted in values is the only vision that will last.
7. Vision makes you a long-term investor, not living for the moment.
8. Goals are the building blocks of vision, vision in work clothes.
9. Model for and teach your children about vision and goals.
10. Opposites attract and men and women are different; identify and admit those differences and use each other's strengths for MORE THAN ENOUGH.
11. Men, build an emergency fund and leave it alone; it will change the way your wife treats you.
12. Budgeting together brings tremendous oneness

to your marriage, but you must die to selfishness; the "you" in "unity" must be silent.

13. Hope is lost when it is placed in people, stuff, and institutions.

14. Hope is lost when we believe failure is permanent and we lose perspective.

15. Hope is an act of the will and moves people to action.

16. Return to strong values and the vision born of them to rekindle your hope.

17. Small groups for support and encouragement are the most powerful form of behavior modification known.

18. When holding your spouse accountable use "I feel" statements that aren't so threatening.

19. Pride busting and encouragement when needed are the lost art of the mentor.

20. To reach **More Than Enough** you have to be as intense as the gazelle is when running from the cheetah: gazelle intensity.

21. Gazelle intensity given focus will create momentum, and momentum in relationships and wealth building brings almost inexplicable illogical things into your life.

8

Good, Better, Best: Work, Discipline, Diligence

Several years ago, Stan, a medicl technician, enrolled in one of our small groups. Stan had been with the same hospital for fourteen years. He made good money, about $60,000 annually, but had a bunch of debt. Within a few weeks, he had come up with a plan that would allow him to be debt free in five months. He was very disciplined and during our small group sessions didn't have too much mercy for the people who had fallen on hard times.

Then one night, six weeks into the program, Stan came in and sat down looking like he had been shot. He didn't sit quite so straight and didn't seem to have all the answers. Just before we were to break he spoke up. He had been laid off that day without notice. He had done nothing wrong; it was just corporate restructuring and his head rolled. Fourteen years of dedication and hard work, and he wasn't even given a single dollar of severance pay, just "hit the door." As he told this story tears began to roll down his cheeks.

"I was on track to be debt free in just five months and now instead I am a crisis case. How will I pay my rent, my electricity. How will I eat?" he sobbed.

We prayed with Stan that night, feeling his shock along with him. Trudi, one of the other participants in the group recommended he get a part-time job just to occupy him and to keep the biggest wolves away from the door.

Stan must have heard Trudi because by the next week's session, he had three part-time jobs. During the day, he was working on a construction site for a temp service. He had taken on a paper route, delivering papers in the mornings, starting at 3 A.M. and again in the afternoons. After the afternoon paper route he delivered pizza until ten o'-clock at night. Just a few hours sleep and he was at it again. He told us that with these three jobs, he could keep his bills current, and stay on track to be out of debt in five months. Four weeks later he got a new job with a different hospital making $15,000 per year more than he did before. He never skipped a beat. Why? Hard work, that's why.

"Work keeps us from three evils: boredom, vice, and poverty," Voltaire said. Why do people believe they can build wealth or relationships without work? I am baffled when I meet so many people who appear intelligent, seem to have hope, and yet the idea of hard work does not even occur to them. They don't shun work or have some idea or theory as to how to avoid work, but working hard, working a lot, just does not occur to them. In Mark 14:7 Jesus said, "The poor will always be with you," and I am convinced that is because there are some people who just don't know how to work. No, everyone who is poor is not poor because they are lazy; there can be other reasons. But one sure way to be poor is to have your antennae turned to something other than work.

WORK IS DOING IT

Work is doing it. Discipline is doing it every day. Diligence is doing it well every day. It all starts with work. Work is where you put clothes on your ideas and walk them down the street. Work is another of the common denominators of people who win. You cannot be the best, you cannot build wealth, you cannot be or do anything of significance if you won't work and work hard. The only lazy or slothful folks who are wealthy are folks who inherited money or won it, and they are rare. Of America's millionaires 80 percent are first-generation rich. That means they got up, left the cave, killed something, and drug it home. If you want to be wealthy and have fabulous relationships, work has to be part of your life.

At other times I meet folks who are going to "pray about their situation." I believe in prayer and I pray daily, but an amazing number of people believe that prayer is all they have to do. St. Ambrose said, "Work like it all depends on you and pray like it all depends on God." An old farmer's proverb says, "Pray for a good harvest, but continue to hoe." Prayer is vital, but God is not in the business of rewarding the lazy.

IT WON'T KILL YOU

Work is one of those paradoxes of life where you think it will result in your being dog-tired all the time when in reality work energizes you. Having something that matters and laying your hand to it gives you energy. Take the case of Whitney, a young woman in her twenties married to an aspiring writer, who had just sold his first novel to a publisher based on only fifty pages of a manuscript. The sale of Doug's novel was a dream come true and they made the decision that the future of his writing career depended on his finishing his book in the next twelve months—something he could do only if he got an unpaid leave of absence from his job as a librarian at a local law firm. Whitney had a very good job as an assistant at a local magazine, but the pay wasn't the greatest—only $22,000 a year. In order to compensate for the loss of Doug's income, Whitney decided she had to take on extra work; she got a job at a local book-store working two evenings a week and on the weekends and got herself several free-lance writing assignments. The twelve months were hard: She and Doug had less time to spend with each other and Whitney always felt as if she were on the run. But she learned an important lesson as well: "I realized I felt so alive and energized by everything I had to do. And the fact is that having more to do outside of my regular job actually made me more productive in my job." After Doug finished his novel and went back to work for the law firm, she decided that she could ease up again, so she quit the bookstore. She also decided to keep doing freelance writing because she had come to cherish the energy and excitement she got from working hard at something she cared about.

Whitney isn't unique, but she is unusual. Over the years, I have counseled people who, if they exerted the same energy on actually doing the task at hand as they do in trying to find some sophisticated way around it, would complete the task. If you spend your day looking for easy work, you will still go to bed worn out. Just do it. I am all for planning and brainstorming, but there comes a point when you get paralysis of the analysis and you actually lose energy. Sometimes you have to say, "Enough! I have to kill something." Posturing is not work, and looking good is not work; you cannot confuse activity with accomplishment. George Kirkpatrick says, "Nature gave us two ends—one to sit on and one to think with. Ever since then man's success or failure has been dependent on which one he used most."

Work completed well brings a sense of satisfaction. The more mature you are the longer you can wait for the satisfaction that completion brings. Children need to feel the closure and the pride quickly. A really mature adult can work on a project months or even years with small notches of completion satisfaction along the way. We feel better about ourselves when we are accomplishing things. It sounds a little sick, but that is the one thing I like about cutting grass. When you are through, in just a few hours, you can step back and see your accomplishment—the yard looks great. Teddy Roosevelt said, "Far and away the best prize that life offers is the chance to work hard at work worth doing."

When times get hard, the bills are overdue, the kids are sick, and you get downsized, you can lose your hope and energy to fight. One sure cure to hard times is work and lots of it. As one sage said, "There are generally four things you can do with your hands: *(1)* put them in your pocket for safekeeping; *(2)* fold them in apathy; *(3)* wring them in despair; or *(4)* lay them on a job that needs doing."

I have heard it said that the reason worry kills more people than work is that more people worry than work. I used to work with a guy who would tell his coworkers that we shouldn't worry about dying from overwork: "When you are worn out, you have been going seven days a week, twenty-five hours a day, when your last shred of energy is gone, you have come to the end of your rope; just before you die you'll pass out, but you won't die." Hard work claims very few victims. You don't have time or brain power to worry when you are focused on work. Another neat thing happens during hard times: When you work, you make money. Work is a surefire moneymaking scheme.

Hard work opens locked doors. The key to almost any locked door is hard work. Hard work seems to surround itself with its friends: opportunity, luck, and solutions to life's greatest problems. The activity created by sheer movement stirs up wonderful things in your life. Real results that are unseen move in your direction just because you stir in God's soup when you work. Margaret Thatcher, the Iron Lady, says, "I do not know anyone who has gotten to the top without hard work. That is the recipe." Thomas Jefferson agreed: "I'm a great believer in luck, and the harder I work the more I have of it." When opportunity knocks you have to be ready not just to answer, but to apply tons of effort to making your chance happen. When you get your shot don't wait on someone else to pull the wagon. If you wait on people to pull your wagon they will all stand and look at the wagon with you. When opportunity knocks don't be surprised if it is wearing work clothes when you answer the door.

DISCIPLINE IS DOING IT EVERY DAY

Work is doing it. Discipline is doing it every day. When you mature into work it actually becomes discipline: doing it *every day.* Discipline understands that get rich quick is a joke. Discipline understands that the best way to get rich quick is to get rich slow. Discipline understands Proverbs 28:20: "A faithful man will abound with blessings: *But he who hastens to be rich will not go unpunished.*"

THE POWER OF DISCIPLINED INVESTMENTS

Building wealth is almost impossible without discipline. I hate this because I too am human and discipline is not easy for me either. But facts are facts and most wealthy people get that way by living on a monthly spending plan, by saving money every month, and by investing money every month. If Ben saves just $100 per month from age twenty-two to age seventy-two at 12 percent in a decent mutual fund he will have $3,905,833. If he saves that amount in a Roth IRA this young man retires with almost $4 million tax free. For the price of a couple of pizzas and cable every month $4 million seems like a deal. There is no excuse to retire broke in America today! But he has to do it *every* month. And so do you.

Maybe you aren't twenty-two anymore; neither am I. You better start now. Start saving and investing now. Discipline is the middle name of the wealthy. In his book, *The Wealthy Barber*, David Chilton sums it well by saying, "The best time to plant an oak tree is twenty years ago, the next best time is now."

It not only takes discipline to invest every month it takes discipline to leave it alone. If you plant an oak tree, water it, fertilize it, and care for it, several years from now it will become a mighty shade tree and a source of great enjoyment to you. But if you pull it up by it's roots every spring to check it's progress it won't live long. Remember Ben who retired with $4 million for $100 per month? Ben has a brother named Dan and Dan did the same thing except he thought he would be sophisticated and remove a down payment for a house from his Roth IRA. Dan removed only $5,000 from his plan when he turned twenty-seven because his broke financial adviser told him that is what the magazines say to do. Dan still put in $100 every month, but that little tinkering caused his retirement fund to sink to $2,828,099. That $5,000 removal at twenty-seven years old cost Dan over $1 million!

A LITTLE TRICKERY GOES A LONG WAY

Since we are all born as savages and have to learn discipline I have a hint. What works best for me, and for most of you, is to go with the flow. The flow is that your nature, like mine, is not disciplined, so you need to remember that when designing your finances. I have found that the best way to handle money properly is to trick yourself into it. First, if your employer offers automatic deposit for your paycheck, use it. I love this option because I don't have to remember to make a trip to the bank. Then when it comes to saving, automatic plans are the best. I have so many mutual funds auto-drafting my checking account each month that it coughs for air around the first of the month. If you have a credit union through your job, you can have them payroll deduct savings to build your emergency fund or Christmas fund. Or if you have a retirement plan that will deduct the money you want to put into it from your paycheck, use it. It is easier to save money that you never see.

You can also have some of your monthly bills auto-drafted. I have all of our utilities, insurance, and even our alarm service auto-drafted. I love the automatic discipline and never missing a discount for paying my bills early.

Never take out a thirty-year mortgage and then promise yourself you will pay extra every month so it will pay off in fifteen years. You may believe that bull, but I have counseled humans for ten years and I know you won't. You will say, "Well, the transmission went out; well, my daughter had to have a prom dress; well, we ran a little short at Christmas; oops, we ran a little over on vacation, *but* we promise to get back on that fifteen-year schedule *next* month." Bull. Besides, the really cool thing about a fifteen-year mortgage is it is always paid off in fifteen years. You will build more wealth if you trick yourself into discipline. Jim Rohn, the motivational speaker, says, "The pain of discipline weighs ounces, but regret weighs tons." Hebrews 12:11 says, "No discipline seems pleasant at the time, but painful. Later on, however, it produces a harvest of righteousness and peace for those who have been trained by it."

TEACH THE CHILDREN

Please teach your kids to work. You doom them to a life of frustration and mediocrity if they don't learn a work ethic from you. Work is a life skill, like bathing, or driving a car, and it must be taught. Babies are cute, but let's face it—they are little savages. Our nature at birth is not a nature that will lead us to prosperity. Our nature must be harnessed and taught. There has never been a child born who gets up every morning, makes his bed, cleans his room, and brushes his teeth—without instruction. By removing work from a child's life you cripple him. That child will enter into the world of adulthood without a clue as to what is coming. Worse yet some poor unsuspecting person may marry this spoiled bum you have raised. Work used to be necessary for survival in America's rural past. You rose before the sun and did chores—hard ones—that brought value to the family, even if you were seven. Character was built at an early age, and this was not child abuse. Child abuse is a little fat boy with his butt in front of the Nintendo for hours on end eating yet another whole bag of Doritos. This child thinks about no one but himself and is in for a long and frustrating life because he has not learned the satisfaction, joy, and value of work.

Start teaching your children the value of work early. At about three years old, they begin to understand how to clean up their toys, and with help and encouragement from a parent they grasp this pretty easily. They can also learn to make a bed, sort of. Straightening the covers counts. Early on, don't obsess about perfection; all you want here is an honest effort, and intent counts a lot. Honestly, in the early years, it is easier to do the work yourself than to have to make a game out of cleaning the room or listening to the complaints about how hard life is on the planet. As you sing songs about cleaning being fun, you are not doing housework, you are doing the work of parenting. As your child completes his work, give him lots of praise. The power of the praise is fun. Have you ever seen a four-year-old little boy throw his shoulders back and walk a little straighter because of a job well done? Work builds self-esteem: "I did it!"

Remember you can't teach your children to work unless you do. A loving father who never failed to involve me in the project of the day taught me my work ethic. By the time I reached college, I not only had the ability to work with my mind, but I could also fix almost anything. I don't always choose to be Mr. Fix-It today, but at least I have a choice. If you don't work hard your children will never learn how to.

Teaching your child useful skills doesn't have to be painful either. Richard recalls the many skills his mother taught him when he was young: "My mother was a neat freak, so it wasn't always fun for me and my four siblings when we had to clean and organize our rooms. But today in my law practice, I really appreciate the things that she taught me about managing my work and my papers." Richard's mother was also a wonderful cook and her kitchen was the center of their home where her children would gather after they had finished their homework or for company on a Saturday afternoon. "She taught each one of us—boys and girls alike—to cook. Today, even ten years after she passed away, it gives me so much pleasure to cook some of the meals she taught me to prepare when I was young and it sure comes in handy with four kids of my own!" Teaching your children to work is also a way of building a meaningful relationship with them, one that will last for years and years—and long beyond the "injustice" of having to do chores.

DON'T MAKE ALLOWANCE

Do not pay allowances to your children. You don't want your children to internalize that everyone should make "allowance" for them. We already have too many people in this country who selfishly believe that. Instead, pay them commissions. Commission means work, get paid; don't work, don't get paid. If the table is not cleaned, or the dog not fed, and Mom or Dad has to catch your slack you get docked some of your pay. In our home, we have three levels of chores. Some chores are mandatory, and the kids have to do them. Some chores are weekly chores that the kids get paid for if they do them, but these are not really optional overall. By that I mean that if one of my kids messes up or has a down week it's OK, but the work will be done most weeks. The third category of chores is totally optional and earns our children bonus pay.

Keep a small, dry-erase or chalkboard on the refrigerator for each child. On the board, list the child's chores and tasks to be done for bonus pay; each week, the child checks off the chores as they are completed. They get paid based on the work they have actually done. The kids will love pay day, especially when all their chores have been checked off throughout the week.

How much should you pay a child for a chore? If your budget can stand it, I suggest that the total weekly commission should equal in dollars about half the child's age. From ages three to six, the commissions should total $1 or $2 a week. As your child grows older you can increase the amount of commission, and the number of chores. By the time your child is seven until about the age of twelve, you might pay as much as $5 per week. At that level, your child should be expected to complete five chores throughout the week; keep the commission schedule simple at $1 per chore per week. As the children reach teen years they should earn from you for different things. One wise friend of mine opened a checking account for his children when they turned fourteen; the children are paid for keeping that account balance to the penny. As they reached their early teens, my daughters baby-sat for their younger brothers or sisters, so our baby-sitting money stayed in the household.

Teens can also earn money outside the home and should be encouraged to do so. Baby-sitting, cutting grass, washing cars, or watching the neighbor's dog can bring in extra money even if they don't get a job with a company. Sometimes teens and even parents get confused about money earned on the outside. The confusion is that the teen earned it so they have the "right" to do whatever they want with that money. Wrong! The teen earned it and should be encouraged to do so, but then it is the parent's job and right to teach the teen how to handle that money. I am not saying you confiscate the money to buy something for yourself. I am saying that you as a parent have a right and an obligation to supervise the use of that money by the teen for his good. "It's my money and I'll do whatever I want with it," only works after you leave home. Proverbs 29:17 says, "Correct your son, and he will give you rest. Yes he will give delight to your soul."

I CAN'T HEAR WHAT YOU SAY,
BUT I'M WATCHING

Teaching your children how to use their money responsibly means teaching them to *save*. If your child is still young, under the age of ten, use a clear plastic jar for saving because young children need visual feedback. A jar full of wadded up dollar bills makes you officially rich. As your child gets older, he should have a savings account. Not all the money he earns has to go into the account, but you and your child should agree on what percentage is going to be saved and stick to it. As with your budget, there may be times when you revise the limit. Perhaps it is Christmastime and your child wants to buy something special for Mom or Dad or a sibling. That is fine, but it should be discussed and talked through before allowing your child to change his savings plan.

The discipline to save for a toy or any hot item is hard when you are three, thirteen, or sixty-three, but it does get easier with practice. There is particular delight when you earn the money, go to the store, select the item, and pay for it. Some poor children never get to experience that level of satisfaction because their parents simply buy them what they want.

There is also real delight when you get to earn money with the sweat of your brow and then use that money to help others by giving. Some children never get to experience that spiritual reward because their parents do what giving is done from their household. You should encourage your children to find ways to give back. The Angel Tree Project, for example, is a wonderful program that provides Christmas gifts to the children of men or women who are serving jail time. At our church and many others across the nation you draw a child's name and what his wish is for Christmas. If you can make that purchase you do so and you wrap the package. A team delivers it before Christmas. It is really cool to watch a child draw a name, buy and wrap the present, to make some other child who they have never seen have a better Christmas. Some of you thought it was a bad idea for me to make children earn money; you thought it was like running some kind of kiddy concentration camp. It's not; the only people you will hurt by avoiding having your children earn money when they are young are your own kids. Some people just don't get it.

A REAL SICKNESS

A sad statistic is emerging in America today. Parents who work hard all their lives building wealth and or building a business are evidently pampering instead of parenting their children. Thomas J. Stanley, who wrote the book *The Millionaire Next Door*, presents some startling statistics about affluent parents "helping" their grown kids too much. Stanley calls this parental assistance economic out-patient care. Parents helping their grown children "get a good start" seem to keep feeding these grown babies into a state of what I call economic dependence. Stupid ideas like "My grandchildren must go to private schools so I'll pay part of the tuition" cripple these grown kids because they never quite cut the apron strings. The rationalization of the parents starts with a noble intent and reaches just plain absurdity as their children arrive at economic dependence. While trying to give them a "good start" is noble, the continued propping up of grown people doesn't have the desired affect. Grown children who are continually given financial gifts are deprived of the need to produce. Grown children receiving gifts have, on average, a net worth of only 80 percent of other people in their same line of work. The offspring of economically codependent parents earn 70 to 80 percent of the income of others in their field. They just aren't hungry enough. Stanley says, "We find that the giving of such gifts is the single most significant factor that explains lack of productivity among the adult children of the affluent."

Teaching your children to work is one of the best gifts a loving parent can give. Don't teach them to depend on you; you will only become frustrated and bitter while your children never really perform at peak.

IT'S NOT JUST THE MONEY

Discipline is a wealth-building key and a key for **MORE THAN ENOUGH** in about every area of your life. A while back I was on an airplane coming home from making one of those author, radio personality, speaker-type appearances. When I fly, I always read, and this time it was a wonderful book called *Halftime* by Bob Buford. Bob challenged me to do what many other speakers and authors have challenged me to do over the years. He challenged me by asking, "If you could change anything in your life what would you change?" Well, I have it made, my life is great these days, but I did an inventory anyway. Marriage, great. Kids, great. Career, great. Books on best-seller lists, great. Radio show with 1 million-plus listeners, great. Investments, great. No debt, great. Wonderful team at my company, great. Then I looked down and lying over the top of the belt line of my pants was this large object, my stomach. Yes, success was showing. I decided right then that it is hypocritical for a fat man to be traveling around the country teaching people how to have discipline.

Because I believe in accountability and support I hired a personal trainer. I knew that if I were paying someone I would show up. I also knew I needed some instruction so I wouldn't be so sore I couldn't walk. Every day I go to the gym and do cardio and weights, and of course I have had to eat less. Yes, discipline does pay off. I feel better and I look better because nine months after that airplane ride I am forty pounds lighter and two and a half inches smaller in my waist. It would be a shame for any of us to have discipline in just one area such as building up wealth and not have the health to enjoy it, the relationships with spouse and family to share it with.

Discipline is a decision and you must make that decision if you want MORE THAN ENOUGH. There is a power and patience to discipline. An old Chinese proverb says, "Be not afraid of growing slowly, be afraid of standing still." You have to decide; discipline is a pure act of your will. Vince Lombardi agreed: "The difference between a successful person and others is not a lack of strength, not a lack of knowledge, but rather a lack of will."

DILIGENCE IS DOING IT EVERY DAY, WELL

Work is doing it. Discipline is doing it every day. Diligence is doing it well every day. Work and discipline are important keys to having **MORE THAN ENOUGH**. Diligence, however, comes with a guarantee. When you are diligent over a long period of time you are guaranteed to become wealthy and have **MORE THAN ENOUGH** in all areas of your life. Diligence is not just showing up or just showing up every day; diligence is showing up every day with excellence. Diligence is when the other keys we have discussed manifest themselves in a real and measurable way. As Proverbs 10:4 says, "He who deals with a slack hand: becomes poor but the hand of the diligent makes one rich."

Diligence has an element of vision to it that tells you a real comfortable place to live is just inside your income. Diligence is knowing that if you can live like no one else can, then you will eventually live like no one else. When you reach a place of diligence in your life you are maturing. Children, whether they are four or fifty-four, are always in a hurry and looking for a shortcut. People who have MORE THAN ENOUGH don't have a shortcut mentality, they think long term. The great opera singer Beverly Sills says, "There is no shortcut to any place that is worth going." A consistent excellence is a rare thing to observe, but so is wealth. Diligence is just that: It is consistent excellence.

Diligence is a trait that makes you read contracts, makes you do research on products and people before you do business with them, and forces you to lay out a plan. I have heard it said that adults devise a plan and follow it, while children do what feels good. Diligence makes you look cradle to grave. People who are diligent with their finances and caring for their family have life insurance, wills, and letters to mates in a pre-agreed file drawer so nothing is lost in the middle of the pain of losing someone.

The cost of not being diligent can be very high. Dorothy went to the office of a mutual fund broker for help with her finances. Her last child was about to move out and she needed advice on investing her $35,000. Dorothy's husband had been killed in a car accident ten years before leaving her a widow with a fourteen- and an eight-year-old to raise. This young widow rolled up her sleeves and made due. She was left with only $35,000 in life insurance money, which placed in a certificate of deposit only paid her about $140 per month. With that as her only income she had been forced to work two and three jobs for the last ten years. Her eight-year-old was now eighteen and made the visit to the mutual fund broker's office with her mom. As he was requested, the broker sold Dorothy her mutual funds to place the $35,000 into and did all the paper work complete with signatures and checks.

As she stood and was about to leave his office Dorothy said, "Oh, I almost forgot I was cleaning out some old files of my husband's in the attic and found these old certificates. Can you tell me what they are?" She pulled from her file some old stock certificates. The broker punched into his computer to try to give her a value. The stock certificates were from pharmaceutical companies and everyone in the room squealed as they discovered they were worth over $800,000. Dorothy was at first overjoyed, then it dawned on her that her husband's lack of planning and diligence had cost her ten years of her life, barely able to feed her children. She was ready to dig him up so she could kill him again. Estate planning is diligence.

DILIGENCE IS DOING THE DETAILS

Long-term care insurance to cover nursing home or in-home care for the elderly is something that diligent planners look at as they reach the age of sixty or so. If you are not that old, you still need to plan diligently. Do you know what situation your parents and your mate's parents will face at retirement? You need to ask them the necessary questions about wills, life insurance, and long-term care insurance.

Wills: Both you and your spouse should have a will, which outlines what is to happen to your major assets—your house and investments, in particular. If you have small children, your will should name the person you have asked to raise them in case of your death.

Life insurance: You should have a policy that pays about ten times your yearly income should you die prematurely. If Joe makes $40,000 per year and leaves his wife Diane and their two kids $400,000 in life insurance, she can invest that $400,000 at 10 percent interest and create $40,000 per year to replace poor Joe. You don't want to buy too much—you'd have to sleep with one eye open.

Long-term care insurance: This covers nursing home care or in-home care and is a good purchase if you have liquid assets under $1 million because otherwise the nursing home bills will destroy your nest egg. You should know where these documents are kept so that you don't end up like Dorothy. Diligence is cradle to grave for you and those around you.

When you teach diligence to children you are teaching them to have vision and to think long term. A very practical tool is to set up a matching arrangement with your children early so they can save for a big item like a car. Agreeing to match what you can afford to is an incentive for them to save and invest. A one for one match is a great reward. As they are working toward their portion of the down payment for the car, you can teach them about different savings and investment options such as a regular savings account or CD. Ask them to calculate the different rates of interest and what difference it will make to their eventual purchase money. At the end of the day, if they save $2,000 and you match it so they can purchase a $4,000 car for cash, you are also teaching them not to incur debt. When you reach this level of diligence in your teaching of preteens and teens they will begin to grasp how powerful investing is. Remember giving them money leads them the wrong way. But giving them character will ensure that they always have money. With the key of diligence in their lives they don't look forlornly at some goal and say with depression in their voices, "I wish I could have one of those or do that." They will know in their bones that they can have or do that if they are willing to pay the price.

Art Williams, who built a huge sales force in the insurance industry, tells the story of the legendary PGA golfer Gary Player. One morning in a practice round Gary teed off with a beautiful long drive right in the center of the fairway. Some guy in the gallery just within Gary's earshot said, "Man I'd give anything to be able to hit a golf ball like you."

Gary walked over to the man and said, "No you wouldn't."

The fan began to argue, saying he really would give anything. Gary explained to the man that there is always a price for excellence.

He said, "You wouldn't do what it takes, because what it takes is you have to rise early in the morning and hit five hundred balls until your hands blister and then begin to bleed. Then you stop, tape your hands, and hit five hundred more balls. The next morning as the sun is rising you are out there again so sore you hobble out with fresh tape and you repeat the scene again. If you do that through enough years of pain you can hit a golf ball like that. You'd love to hit a ball like me, but only if it were easy."

Diligence understands this story because it is diligence that created it.

THIS WILL WORK FOR YOU

To have MORE THAN ENOUGH you must understand consistent excellence, called diligence, and it must be a daily partner of yours. This must be true no matter what you do, as Dr. Martin Luther King, Jr., so wisely said: "If a man is called to be a street sweeper, he should sweep the streets even as Michelangelo painted or Beethoven composed music or Shakespeare wrote poetry. He should sweep streets so well that all the hosts of heaven and earth will pause to say: Here lived a great street sweeper who did his job well."

Are you working as diligently as you can in everything that you do? Stop and take your own inventory as I did on that flight home. Rate each area of your life, circling the response that reflects where you actually are:

Marriage:	excellent	good	okay	not so great
Kids:	excellent	good	okay	not so great
Career:	excellent	good	okay	not so great

Finances:	excellent	good	okay	not so great
Investments:	excellent	good	okay	not so great
Friendships:	excellent	good	okay	not so great
Future				
(wills, insurance, retirement):				
	excellent	good	okay	not so great
Physical:	excellent	good	okay	not so great
_____ :	excellent	good	okay	not so great

It's probably pretty clear to you by looking at this list what areas of your life you need to work on. And if you've circled excellent for everything, that's great, but I bet that, like me, there is something you need to work on. Don't try to overwhelm yourself by trying to fix everything at once; pick one area and think about what work you need to do to improve upon it. Write down your plan and ask your accountability partner to help you stay on track.

If you are a parent, you owe it to your children to teach them about work and about money. You can't change everything overnight—you don't want them to think you've turned into Attila the Hun—but you do need to teach them while they're young. Introduce them to the system of commissions, start on a project around the house with your child as your partner, open a savings account in your child's name, and make them responsible for making regular deposits and keeping the account balanced. The best and most lasting way to teach them is by your example: Work is doing it. Discipline is doing it every day. Diligence is doing it well every day.

THE STORY CONTINUES

Out of core *values, vision* is born. *Vision* is put into work clothes and becomes *goals.* Shared *goals* gives you *unity* with those who are on the journey with you. *Values, vision,* and *unity* repair broken *hope* and build *hope* into the fuel that fires the rocket of *intensity.* The rocket of *intensity* is kept between the ditches by *accountability* and *support.* The pilot of the rocket ensuring that it stays on *vision's* course is *diligence.* His copilot and navigator are *work* and *discipline.*

Thoughts from Sharon . . .

Work is a verb that is used at our house a lot. Work may not always be fun, but it can be rewarding.

It isn't right for parents to feel like they must do everything for their children. Growing up in today's world it's easy to become lazy. I don't want the word lazy to be used in our household. It's like Dave says: You work, you get paid; you don't work, you don't get paid.

As a teenager, I grew up in a household like Dave's. My father owned a store and in the summer it was understood, no matter what, that we helped out. There were many days I wished I could sleep late or go to the pool. But I knew that my dad was depending on me to help. At the time it was not all fun, but the values it placed in my life are now fond memories with no regrets.

We are teaching our children that they cannot expect others to always be doing things for them. Yes, we nuture them and take care of them, but they know that there are things that they must do for themselves. They must be responsible and learn to work with ethics and integrity the same as we do.

Keys to the More Than Enough Mansion

1. Change is very hard and we change only when the pain of *same* is greater than the pain of change.
2. Cleansing cries and hinge pins are signals that we are ready.
3. Values really do matter and real values are the foundation of everything to come.
4. Integrity—real deep integrity, even with the little things—is vital because deception destroys.
5. Connectedness is key; take time to use the sidewalks that connect you to family, friends, and coworkers.
6. Vision that is rooted in values is the only vision that will last.
7. Vision makes you a long-term investor, not living for the moment.
8. Goals are the building blocks of vision, vision in work clothes.
9. Model for and teach your children about vision and goals.
10. Opposites attract and men and women are different; identify and admit those differences and use each other's strengths for MORE THAN ENOUGH.
11. Men, build an emergency fund and leave it alone; it will change the way your wife treats you.
12. Budgeting together brings tremendous oneness

to your marriage, but you must die to selfishness; the "you" in "unity" must be silent.

13. Hope is lost when it is placed in people, stuff, and institutions.

14. Hope is lost when we believe failure is permanent and we lose perspective.

15. Hope is an act of the will and moves people to action.

16. Return to strong values and the vision born of them to rekindle your hope.

17. Small groups for support and encouragement are the most powerful form of behavior modification known.

18. When holding your spouse accountable use "I feel" statements that aren't so threatening.

19. Pride busting and encouragement when needed are the lost art of the mentor.

20. To reach MORE THAN ENOUGH you have to be as intense as the gazelle is when running from the cheetah: gazelle intensity.

21. Gazelle intensity given focus will create momentum, and momentum in relationships and wealth building brings almost inexplicable illogical things into your life.

22. Work is doing it, discipline is doing it every day, and diligence is doing it well every day.

23. No one has MORE THAN ENOUGH in relationships or wealth without hard work, discipline, and diligence.

9

Patience Is Golden

When Paul and Molly got married, Molly moved into Paul's small bachelor pad. It made sense: Paul's rent was half of what Molly was paying and while the apartment was smaller than Molly's, it wasn't *that* much smaller. The couple had decided they wanted to buy a house, and although each brought some savings to the marriage, it wasn't enough for the down payment for a house in New York City where they lived. Starting a marriage in a small apartment, especially when Paul ran his consulting business from home, provided some definite challenges. Paul had to learn that he couldn't keep the stereo on twenty-four hours a day; Molly had to learn a lot more about baseball than she ever thought she'd want to know; and Paul and Molly had to learn to put every single extra penny they had into their house fund. As time went on they found that they enjoyed watching their nest egg grow, and after about eighteen months they were ready to buy the house of their dreams. As they began their search, they discovered that the real estate market was tighter than it had been in years. People were literally walking into houses and making offers above and beyond the asking price! Houses were selling within days of being put on the market. Finding a house they loved and could afford would be no easy matter. After a few months of looking, Paul suggested that perhaps he should rent office space somewhere so that at least they wouldn't be giving up a third of their space to his business. It was tempting, but together Paul and Molly realized that waiting to find their dream home, without incurring higher monthly costs from additional rent for an office, would mean they would be in a stronger position to buy the home they really wanted when the time came.

All our lives, we have heard that silence is golden. Well, I am here to tell you that patience is golden. In a culture where we all feel like gerbils in a wheel, where we measure speed in megahertz and nanoseconds, we have become time-maximized maniacs. Patience seems like such an old-fashioned virtue. But as Paul and Molly learned as they saved money to buy their dream home, patience has its rewards. Just the word itself feels like peace that we long for. Patience is golden because patience will increase your gold. Patience is golden because it will increase the satisfaction you take from achieving your goals and desires. And patience is golden because it is formed from heat much like pure gold is. To purify gold the goldsmith of old would stoke the fire to bring the gold to a boil, and as the gold boiled the dross, the impurities, would rise to the top. The goldsmith would skim off the junk until he could see himself. Problems that we face, the heat of life, make the junk come to the surface, and God skims the junk out of our lives until He can look at us and see some of Himself. The heat of life adds character and almost always people who have faced extreme adversity have unbelievable patience. Patience is golden because it is born of heat.

IN A CHILD'S REALM

When we go into a store or get the fever to buy something, that Kellogg's kid inside us wakes up—you know, the kid inside who likes the frosting. That kid wakes up every time I go into an electronics store. He is the guy telling me to buy a big screen when all I came for was a pack of batteries. That kid is the one who thought buying that time-share on impulse was a great idea. That kid is the one who tells you to use a credit card and promises you'll be able to pay it off "real quick." I am sure it was that same kid who threw a temper tantrum to get that boat so "the whole family could spend time together." It is probably that kid who would trade in a great marriage and wife for a secretary with a short dress. That kid is inside of every one of us and can cause us to make some really impulsive stupid decisions. These stupid decisions are the kind of decisions that damage our bank account or our relationships.

That kid who lives inside of all of us is immaturity. Childish selfishness that stamps its foot and says, "I want it now!" A lack of patience causes debt, because we say "I need it now," when in reality we just got the fever. We have exchanged the old layaway pay-until-paid plan for a new credit card "lay-awake" plan. Our culture's childish impatience has led us so deeply into debt we can't breathe.

Patience is growing up. Patience knows that one definition of maturity is learning to delay pleasure. Patience prefers a Crock-Pot in a microwave culture. Patience born of maturity will make you rich. It will make you rich in dollars and rich in relationships.

Patience is willing to let intensity have time to create momentum. Patience is willing to be diligent over a period of time, even a long time, to get to the goal our vision laid out for us. Patience will cause you to build wealth because you are willing to save and pay cash instead of borrow. When you don't have any payments it is easy to save and invest enough to become wealthy in just a few years. Think about it: If you are bringing home $2,000 a month and your food, clothing, utility, and housing costs only add up to $1,500 a month, you have $500 left over to divide between pleasure and savings. On the other hand, if you have credit card debt and a car loan and have to pay $350 a month just to meet the minimum payments in addition to your $1,500 monthly costs, you have only $150 left over for pleasure activities and savings. And how much are you really going to save out of that $150 each month? You may look at this scenario and think, "Well, I'm making my payments and still have money left over each month, so what's the problem?" The problem is that you didn't use the power of patience; you took short-term pleasure ahead of long-term smarts. With patience, you would have put off buying that new car until you could pay cash; you wouldn't have squandered your future just so you could have that gleaming new machine that started depreciating the minute you drove it off the car dealer's lot.

KEEP YOUR WEALTH

Patience allows you to keep your wealth because it makes you decide what something is worth to you—and stick to it. It makes you a great bargain hunter. The best way to get great bargains is to maintain your "walk-away power." There is tremendous negotiating power in being able to wait. When you do not have the buying fever you act differently in the buying process and you tend to get deeper discounts. Sometimes the patience it takes to simply be quiet for a moment while on the phone with a potential seller will cause a discussion to turn your way. It takes a very confident person with no signs of buying fever to simply let a pause in the conversation lay. The pressure and drama that are created by silence born of patience will make you money in negotiations. Obviously being able to hold out and continue to shop for the best deal will also make you money. By being patient and not allowing the buying fever to catch you, you force the seller to catch the fever—the selling fever. Instead of making a decision to spend $1,000 more than you decided to because "I'm so close I can just see that brand new SUV in the driveway," you force the seller to drop his price $1,500 dollars because if he doesn't sell to you, "I won't make my monthly quota, and who else will buy this car?"

Of course patience also applies to saving. Remember the brothers—Ben who left his money alone and Dan who pulled only $5,000 out early, which cost him over $1 million in his nest egg? That lack of patience made a huge difference in Dan's net worth. Patience is continuing to save every month after every month. Patience is not touching monies that are earmarked for retirement or your kid's college fund, ever.

Kind of reminds me of that old Aesop's fable "The Goose with the Golden Egg." You remember, the farmer and his wife have a goose laying golden eggs, one per day. At the rate of one per day they were becoming steadily wealthy. Greed kicked in and they decided that if they killed the goose they could get all the gold out of the inside and not have to wait. Of course the goose had no gold inside, she was just a regular goose. So they had no more eggs and no more goose, because (now you remember) they had killed the goose that laid the golden egg.

TAG, YOU ARE IT

Patience and endurance play tag. You will always find one where the other has been. Endurance through tough times always increases your measure of patience. Patience is also strength of character, which gives you the ability to endure. Patience that can endure is true power.

Have you ever watched the Tour de France? For three weeks the best cyclists in the world race every single day on a course that takes them throughout the country: in the mountains and on the flats, in rain or shine, as teams within the pelathon (the main pack of cyclists), and as individuals during two time trials when the riders race against the clock. It's a race that requires incredible strength and endurance and every year only about 70 percent of those who start finish. The 1998 tour had a living example of how patience, endurance, and strength of character work together to create winners. The tour was won by a young Italian rider, Marco Pantani, known as the Pirate. He beat the defending champion, Jan Ullrich, in an extraordinary race in which he attacked in the most mountainous part of the course. The Pirate built up enough of a lead in three critical days in the French Alps that he was able to win the entire race.

Pantani's victory was especially amazing because three years earlier, he had had a career-threatening accident. On October 18, 1995, during the Turin Race in Italy, the Pirate was racing downhill and crashed into a car. Can you imagine sitting atop your bicycle, speeding downhill at more than 30 mph, and going headfirst into a car? Pantani suffered grave injuries, including smashing one of his legs, with a break so severe no one knew whether he'd ever be able to walk again, much less ride a bike. He spent months and months going through agonizing physical therapy to regain the strength in his leg, not to mention having to be patient enough to fight off the fear of not knowing whether he would ever be able to compete again in a sport he loved and excelled at. But Marco Pantani did race again and in 1998 won not only the Tour de France, but also the Tour of Italy—one of only thirteen men ever to have accomplished this feat. Now, that's the power of patience and endurance! Those with the most power in the patience category seem to endure with the most class and with the most ease.

PATIENCE IS NOT JUST ABOUT MONEY

Patience born of endurance is the kind that cares more about relationships and long-term issues like integrity, so it changes the way you treat people. Patience is a fruit of your trials, and that kind of patience becomes golden when it touches your relationships. Remember the goldsmith and the impurities He is removing, when looking for His image? Part of what He sees is patience while He skims off immaturity and selfishness. You will rarely meet someone with patience rooted in power who has not seen heavy trials. I don't wish bad times for you, but if you are in them I can promise you if you work through the tough times one natural occurrence is that your level of patience will be increased.

Chuck Swindoll, one of the nation's best-loved preachers, says God answers all prayers. His answer can be yes, or no, or grow. Sometimes your heavenly Father sees you in the fire and like that goldsmith, allows that boiling action to clean impurities from you. When He looks into the gold, you, and sees His image a little clearer he douses the fire. Never fear that the fire can be too hot because He has his hand on the thermostat.

You have heard of the patience of Job, the character in the Bible with serious hard times. Patience that is the fruit of endurance gives you an increased ability to respond to life, rather than react to it. After you have been in the soup a few times you tend to be not quite so selfish, so your relationships are given a priority You can become a peacemaker. If you view long-term relationships and results as more important than petty personal turf, it turns you into a master consensus builder. We are not talking about a patience of weakness, which is simply stalling, putting off making a hard decision. This is a patience that considers all the people involved, their agendas, and their best interests, then has the power and personal courage to make the decision.

When I was a young and brash character with all the answers, I was a member of a leadership team for a volunteer organization. The leader who ran the organization assembled a team of very confident and competent people. As you might guess, putting all these high-powered guns in one room to set vision and approve budgets can cause casualties. People can be vicious especially when protecting turf or trying to make a high-powered point. I learned a lot on that team, but by far the most valuable lesson was about patience's role in leadership. Our leader had patience born of experience that gave him the ability to mold his team into a consensus. Some of our meetings were "too long," but everyone there got to play and have his say; and we hammered the problem at hand until everyone understood one another's position. We would have a consensus before we moved on or we wouldn't move on. The personal power shown by our leader as he waited until we'd all gotten through our junk, until the positions and issues could be molded into a solution, brought a respect and a unity to that team that was incredible. We always left the meeting with a loyalty to the organization, each other, and our leader that was the direct result of his patience.

In our culture where hard-driving "get things done" Type-A people are those we honor and attempt to model our success after, patience doesn't seem to have a place. True success has an element of patience that gives the person walking with it the peace to make long-term decisions with the view of a mountaintop. Perspective comes from patience. When you meet one of these people don't mistake them for indecisive boobs or cowards who don't have the spine to make the tough call. They can make the call, but only when patience tells them that people and long-term values have been considered and protected. They have a different perspective than some young hotshots. They will always value people, consensus, agreement, the team, values, and the long-term effects of the decision over posturing or the perception of others.

Patience is having the nobility to wait because the result is more important than personal pleasure in the meantime. How do you develop this kind of patience? One way, the hard way, is to go through trials. I don't like pain as a teacher, but if you are in that school, make sure the lesson is learned so you don't have to go back for another semester. Another way is to make a commitment to developing patience and follow through with it. How can you do that? Start by thinking about what area of life you need to learn patience in. Ask yourself the following questions and circle the answer that most applies to you:

1. Am I a good saver and investor? yes / no
2. Do I listen to my spouse even when I'm dog-tired and want to relax in front of the TV? yes / no
3. When one of my coworkers needs help, do I stop what I'm doing to explain how to finish the project? yes / no
4. Do I share my time with my kids doing any of the things *they* want to do with me? yes / no
5. When I want something that I can't yet afford, do I wait until I have saved the money it will cost before I buy it? yes / no

I could have given you an easy way out and given you "sometimes" as an option, since most of us are usually someplace between yes and no. But you need to take a hard, honest look at yourself without an easy out to be able to really focus on where you need to learn patience. Go back and look at the questions where you answered no;

those are the areas you need to work on in the patience arena.

If you aren't saving, go back to your budget and find a way to save at least $50 a month, every month. If you need help with this, ask your accountability partner to work through your budget with you or to keep you focused on laying your own golden egg.

If you aren't listening to your spouse, sit down tonight for at least twenty minutes to talk and listen. Remember to listen—even if you don't care about the curtains she wants to buy (or the latest bit of gossip from his office). Choose one night each week when the two of you will forgo TV and listen to each other. Learn the count-to-five rule: Before you snap or tell your spouse she doesn't know what she's talking about, count to five, slowly.

If you haven't been a good colleague, take the time and energy to help a colleague the next time you are asked. Try mentoring a young member of the staff whose lack of knowledge may be frustrating, but teaching them will reward you with the gift of patience and gratitude.

If you never, or rarely, let your kids decide how they will spend their time with you, let them plan next Saturday's activities. Obviously their choice must be age appropriate and fit into your budget, but if it means you have to sit through the movie *Madeline* or spend two hours catching them as they come down the slide at the park or playing dolls with them, do it. Try letting the kids plan one Saturday a month. Yes, you may end up sitting through some activities you'd rather not, but you will not only learn patience, you will also gain years of memories and shared time with your children.

If you can't wait to buy, go look in your folder of bills. I'm betting you have credit card debt or car payments: Sit down and figure out how to pay them off. You will not buy anything except for necessities until you are debt free. If you have no debt and you want to make a significant purchase that you can't pay cash for, don't, yet. Sit down and figure out how much you need to save per week to buy that item you want. In each of these cases, you should get your accountability partner involved in making the decisions and sticking to them.

These small lessons won't make you patient overnight, but they will help you to start along patience's path. And believe me, it's a lot better to have to learn this lesson without graduating from the school of hard knocks as I have. I have learned that if I stop and adjust things like patience and the perception it brings then a special kind of personal power becomes mine. Personal power born of patience has such a depth and strength to it that you can't help but be wiser and kinder: wiser about your financial planning and investing; wiser about your relationships at home, at work, and within your community; wiser about how you spend your time; kinder in your dealings with your family, friends, and neighbors; kinder in the way you treat the people who work for and around you; kinder in your attitudes toward those with less patience than you. This wisdom and kindness will cause More Than Enough to happen in wealth and relationships.

THE STORY CONTINUES

Out of core *values, vision* is born. *Vision* is put into work clothes and becomes *goals.* Shared *goals* give you *unity* with those who are on the journey with you. *Values, vision,* and *unity* repair broken *hope* and build *hope* into the fuel that fires the rocket of *intensity.* The rocket of *intensity* is kept between the ditches by *accountability* and *support.* The pilot of the rocket ensuring that *intensity* stays on *vision's* course is *diligence.* His copilot and navigator are *work* and *discipline. Patience* that is born of power has its center *intensity, hope, vision,* and *diligence.* You can't have real *patience* without first having those things and when you have it relationships are built and you add yet more *unity.*

Thoughts from Sharon . . .

You've heard it before, patience is a virtue. If you wait long enough, whatever you're waiting for may end up being better than you thought.

Patience in adults can help you mature fast. Children need to be taught patience because otherwise they would grow up to be spoiled and selfish. We need to pray for patience, and I do that often.

Here's an example of how if you have patience; you will be glad you waited. Dave and I moved to Williamson County because of the school system. Because we decided to move the week school started, we had to rent a house, knowing we would have plenty of time to look for the house we wanted to buy. Well, six months turned into two full years. You talk about someone who was running out of patience! Me! Constantly I was being told to just have a little patience and you'll get the house of your dreams. The kids and I prayed every night for three things we wanted in our new house (a white kitchen, a big backyard with lots of trees, and a three-car garage). I know that doesn't sound like much to some of you, but to us those were some very important details. After two full years of having patience we finally found exactly what we were praying for and even more.

To this day Dave reminds me of that two-year wait and how having patience is what got us our dream house. Try it; you'll see the difference in the decisions you make.

Keys to the More Than Enough Mansion

1. Change is very hard and we change only when the pain of *same* is greater than the pain of change.
2. Cleansing cries and hinge pins are signals that we are ready.
3. Values really do matter and real values are the foundation of everything to come.
4. Integrity—real deep integrity, even with the little things—is vital because deception destroys.
5. Connectedness is key; take time to use the sidewalks that connect you to family, friends, and coworkers.
6. Vision that is rooted in values is the only vision that will last.
7. Vision makes you a long-term investor, not living for the moment.
8. Goals are the building blocks of vision, vision in work clothes.
9. Model for and teach your children about vision and goals.
10. Opposites attract and men and women are different; identify and admit those differences and use each other's strengths for MORE THAN ENOUGH.
11. Men, build an emergency fund and leave it alone; it will change the way your wife treats you.
12. Budgeting together brings tremendous oneness

to your marriage, but you must die to selfishness; the "you" in "unity" must be silent.

13. Hope is lost when it is placed in people, stuff, and institutions.

14. Hope is lost when we believe failure is permanent and we lose perspective.

15. Hope is an act of the will and moves people to action.

16. Return to strong values and the vision born of them to rekindle your hope.

17. Small groups for support and encouragement are the most powerful form of behavior modification known.

18. When holding your spouse accountable use "I feel" statements that aren't so threatening.

19. Pride busting and encouragement when needed are the lost art of the mentor.

20. To reach MORE THAN ENOUGH you have to be as intense as the gazelle is when running from the cheetah: gazelle intensity.

21. Gazelle intensity given focus will create momentum, and momentum in relationships and wealth building brings almost inexplicable illogical things into your life.

22. Work is doing it, discipline is doing it every day, and diligence is doing it well every day.

23. No one has MORE THAN ENOUGH in relationships or

wealth without hard work, discipline, and diligence.

24. Patience is golden and like gold is purified in the fires of life.

25. Patience brings real power to your wealth building and a real quality to your relationships because you are looking long term.

26. Patience makes you an investor who stays in the market and reaps long-term rewards, and patience demands you save to pay cash so you avoid debt.

10

Looking for Love in All the Wrong Places

There is a gift that causes blessings to flow to anyone who possesses it. If you have this gift it will lead to your heart's every desire. Over the years of observing the unusual behavior and the insight of people who have **MORE THAN ENOUGH**, I have found they have all obtained this gift. I would venture to say that if you can acquire this gift it may very well be the most powerful financial gift you can have. If you can grasp this concept, take ownership of it, and make it a part of your very being, you can have virtually anything. This gift is so powerful that when you get it you can get completely out of debt very quickly. If you possess this gift you can give like you have always wanted to give. If you count this gift among your assets you will be able to save and invest like others only dream of. Those who have this gift, who have lived this principle, have lives truly filled with **MORE THAN ENOUGH**. I rarely find winners in the game of life who have great relationships and have built wealth unless they have at least some degree of this gift functioning in their lives. The happiest people you will ever meet have this gift in abundance, and they seem to be almost eerie. They have a sense of density and perspective that is so deep it will almost spook you. I think that we are spooked because we meet very few people who have a deep use and sense of this gift. I really do believe that this is possibly the most powerful financial principal. What is this magnificent principal, this gift from on high? *Contentment.*

When you have contentment you can easily get out of debt. When you have contentment you can easily save and invest. When you are content it changes your giving habits and your relationships. When you are content it brings an inner strength that will push you into another zone. You are able to move fast or slow, and you are able to have patience or intensity when you are content. Contentment is a magnificent personal gift.

In our society designed and ruled by hard-driving type As we have actually twisted the definition of contentment. Contentment is viewed as something for some hippie flower child or some drug zombie or is the curse of the lazy. Contentment is not apathy and yet we often confuse the two. We have become adrenaline addicts in the ever-growing pursuit of the bigger and the better. We believe you should get all you can and can all you get.

THE REAL FUN BEGINS

In this gerbil-in-a-wheel culture if you have true, deep abiding contentment, you are weird—a good weird. Because normal is stressed out, you are spooky to others. The fun thing for me has been to watch people learn to develop contentment. My fun really kicks in when I get to watch the power that their newfound contentment has to improve their relationships and help them build wealth. Relationships prosper when you have peace and are able to serve those you love most. You can't really serve and enjoy those around you if you are emotionally or spiritually needy. Contentment is only born of strength.

In the seventies we all became enamored with *Star Wars* and the adventures of Luke Skywalker. The Force led Luke to Jedi training with the famous Jedi Master, Yoda. Turns out the best trainer in the universe is a big-eared, bug-eyed, little lizardlike dwarf who lived in a terrible swamp with almost no visible assets to his name. As we watched Yoda train young Luke we all realized this character had an inner strength that was modeled after those from a couple of generations before us who valued character, relationships, and contentment above the chase of stuff. We were drawn to those values and came to admire the little lizard. Before that we were drawn to the inner peace and simplicity of a TV series called *Kung Fu*. This guy wasn't motivated by stuff, seemed to have it together, and yet could kick some tail if needed. We were drawn to those values. I'm not saying that I endorse *Kung*

Fu or *Star Wars*, but it is interesting to note how we were drawn to the roles played that represented contentment and a quiet inner strength.

Building wealth really can take on a whole new look and speed when it doesn't matter quite so much anymore. As I have watched folks win from developing contentment I became a student of what steals our contentment and how to get a new heavy dose of it in our lives. In our macho, hyper culture, we've mistaken contentment for weakness, rather than seeing it for what it really is: born of strength.

Let me introduce you to two couples who came into our offices not long ago. Couple number one has an annual household income of $35,000 and at forty years old they have $150,000 in their 401(k) plan with no personal debt on cars or credit cards. And they are on track to pay off their $70,000 home in just three more years. They have savings for emergencies and go on paid-for vacations with their family every year. Couple number two comes in with $64,000, not in savings, but in credit card debt. They have no savings, two very nice cars that are leased, a ten-year-old student loan, and a $175,000 home on an adjustable rate mortgage because that is the only way they could qualify. Did they create this mess because they make less than the first couple's $35,000 per year? No, these folks have a household income of over $84,000 per year! What is it that causes one couple to be able to prosper on an annual income of $35,000 while the other is heading toward bankruptcy with over $84,000 in yearly income?

It's easy to say that the difference between couple number one and couple number two is contentment, but what does that really mean? It doesn't mean that we are satisfied with what we have. It does mean that building wealth takes on a whole new look and speed when it doesn't matter quite so much anymore. The truth is that the best way to learn about what contentment is, is to become a student of what steals our contentment.

SOLD TO THE MAN IN THE CHECKERED PANTS

I've said it before and I'll say it again: We live in the most marketed-to society in the history of the world. We are sold to, talked at, marketed to, and advertised to, at a rate of literally thousands of exposures a day. Radio, television, print, billboards, and even public restroom walls scream product and service offers at a brain-rattling pace. The level of sophistication and repetition at which we are pitched to is enough to cause serious psychosis, and some argue it already has. Frogs selling beer, pantyhose hatching from eggs, Beanie Babies in McDonald's Happy Meals, sports figures pitching bill consolidation, and small dogs marketing tacos are enough to make you wonder what's next. Superstores that seem to be entire cities under one roof, warehouse stores with "great" buys, triple coupon days when Jupiter aligns with Mars, and billions and billions served—is there an end? "The real thing."

"It's the right way, Baby." "Have it your way." And if you close your eyes and think real hard on a hot summer's day you too can fly off a tire swing into the swimming hole. We are so pummeled by marketing techniques and strategies to grab our ever-shrinking spendable dollar that our collective heads are spinning. Is advertising and marketing evil? No, in fact, I have always loved to sell, so very early on I became a student of people so I could do a better job at it.

In sales training classes, I was taught that most people go through several steps before making a purchase. First, we recognize a perceived need or want. Once we decide that this item or service will bring us more pleasure or help us avoid pain, we begin to make mental calculations toward the purchase. When these calculations are in their last stages, we then start to visualize our ownership after the purchase. When this emotional ownership takes place, we wake up from our daydream to realize we haven't yet made ownership a reality and that frustrates us. This frustration builds and builds to a boiling point and just before total explosion we buy. We are really agitated right at the moment of purchase and immediately begin to calm afterward. The more expensive the purchase the more frustrated we become just before the deal is sealed. This progressive process happens whether we buy a candy bar or a house. The recognition of the frustration process happens very quickly, and we don't even notice it when the price is small or the purchase is not important, like a candy bar. However, when we buy a home or a new car, propose marriage, or purposefully conceive and have children, the progression that ends in high frustration is very real.

Professional marketers and advertisers understand that they have to point out a need to you so you will recognize a need you didn't know you had. When you recognize that need, the process we just talked about has started and will end in frustration and finally purchase if the marketer did his job well. Back in Psych 101, we were taught the concept of "dissonance," which basically means disturbance. When someone recognizes a way to get more pleasure or avoid pain they are moved, motivated, in that direction. The thing that moves or motivates us is this disturbance or dissonance. If you are a good marketer or advertiser your job is to bring dissonance or a disturbance to the person receiving your message. When the marketer disturbs you, then you will recognize your new need or want, which leads you to a level of frustration until the deal is sealed. That is the essence of marketing, to create an emotional disturbance.

Some of these disturbances are even pleasant, but we do not move, we are not motivated by anything other than a disturbance. Juliet B. Schor, in her book *The Overspent American*, states that her research shows that each added hour of television viewing increases a consumers spending by roughly $200 per year. So an average level of TV watching of fifteen hours per week equals nearly $3,000 extra spent per year. When you consider a study by A. C. Nielsen Co. that says in 1996 Americans watched

250 billion hours of TV, the overspending as a culture is incredible. What this study shows us is that the more we are pummeled with ads the more we buy, chasing that brass ring of happiness around our own little gerbil wheel. Living in the most marketed-to civilization in history means we are systematically having our contentment stolen. All of this disturbance has lead us to be a very discontented people. This discontent is taking our wealth and our relationships.

SIGNS, SIGNS, EVERYWHERE A SIGN

There are several signs that point to someone who is discontented. One thing folks do if they lack contentment is they are always looking for a shortcut. They fall for get-rich-quick scams and schemes. When someone doesn't have contentment he is always in a hurry to get it all and get it all right now. There is a reason your mom told you not to run in the house, because when you run where you should be walking you will fall and hurt yourself. Folks who don't have contentment are always jumping from job to job; they are always looking for that BBD, that bigger better deal. They start businesses on an impulse, and their garages are full of the trophies of discontent. The trophies are the remains of failed ideas that were going to send them straight to the top. The boxes of unsold products, the vending machines that didn't work out, and the used office equipment from the failed business. Don't get me wrong, I have sold these trophies from my own garage too. A valid attempt that fails is different from a life full of get-rich-quick schemes that didn't work.

Get-rich-quick thinking is not the only signal that you have missed the contentment boat. The need to appear rich quick is also a sign. Most of us have this problem as young adults. Twentysomethings are more concerned about labels and being identified with brands than any previous generation. But I see all ages fall for the look or the label trap. We emotionally need to appear to be something we have not yet become. It is this lack of contentment that causes us to buy things we can't afford, and we end up deeply in debt, all for the sake of appearance. Appearing rich before we are is a sign of discontentment that is widespread in our whole society. I have heard it said that "thousands upon thousands of people are yearly brought into a state of real poverty by their great anxiety not to be thought poor." When the money runs out, and it always does because there is never enough money if you don't have contentment, our "luck" seems to leave with the money. We buy things we don't even know how to turn on or operate properly and by the time we finally get them paid for we hate them. We hate them because every time we go near them they shout at us about our impulsiveness and immaturity.

Worry and fear are everywhere. Worry and fear are another sign that contentment is not in the house. Worry and fear paralyze us and have reached truly epidemic levels in our culture. Worry and fear cannot exist in the same house as contentment does. When we are disturbed and frustrated by our finances and/or our relationships, worry and fear live with us day and night. Oh, those long nights that worry brings to so many.

The last and one of the most often seen signs of contentment not being in the house is envy. Of course *you* have never envied what someone had, but maybe you have this friend. . . . Wanting the stuff, success, or even relationships of others is normal and we all do it from time to time. The grass is always greener under someone else's teepee. But the fact is that we can never really know the reality of other people's lives. That couple with the gorgeous house on the corner you'd die to have? They probably were in my office last week for financial counseling. The Ken and Barbie in your circle, whose marriage seems so perfect? You just learned they were in marriage counseling. James Ferarr, an author who writes on family issues, talks about our culture that worships *Better Homes and Gardens*. Better than whose? Better than mine? It can't be better than mine!

Envy and this sick need to have what someone else has will never make us happy. He with the most toys when he dies is dead. Remember the old preacher's joke: You never see a Ryder truck following a hearse. That's because you can't take it with you, and having things you can't yet afford won't make you any happier when you're alive either.

I'LL BE HAPPY WHEN . . .

Joe Land, a motivational speaker, talks about this lack of contentment and how it can cause us to chase happiness. Joe says that we can all remember being in kindergarten, and in his talks tells of a progression that we have all observed: the I'll-be-happy-when syndrome.

Take the case of my son who graduates to first grade this year. He really believes just like you and I did that he'll be "happy" when he gets to first grade where they finish teaching him how to read. "Next year, Dad, I'll be in a grade with a number on it," he told me the other day. But when you finally get into first grade, you find out there are these really cool dudes up at the top of the mountain called sixth graders. You say, "I'll be 'happy' when I get to sixth grade." When you get to sixth grade you want to go to middle school where you change classes and have a locker. "I'll be 'happy' when" I get to middle school. In middle school your friend has an older brother in high school and he has a driver's license. In high school you can drive and go out on dates. "I'll be 'happy' when I get to high school." Then when you get to high school that same older brother comes home from college. He tells all about how cool college is: "They don't even care if you go to class in college." "Wow, I'll be 'happy' when I get to college." You finally get to college and you live on an average checking balance of $1.67 and a box of No-Doze and think to yourself, "If I could just get out of here." You think, "I can't wait to get a real job, meet that special someone, get married, have 2.3

kids and a house with a white picket fence just like in *Leave It to Beaver*. I'll be 'happy' then." You get out of college, get married; the stresses of family start and you think, "I want to go back to college." Those diapers need to be changed and you promise yourself you'll be "happy" when the last one is potty-trained. You blink and those kids are teenagers and you are sure you'll be "happy" when they leave. They leave and get married and you call them every day wanting to know when they are going to make you into Granny and Papa so you can change diapers again. "I'll be happy then." Happiness is like the bully on the schoolyard: He draws a line in the sand and dares you to cross it. When you cross the line he backs up and draws another, daring you to cross that. If you don't find happiness where you are, you will never find it.

We get caught up in thinking, "I'll be 'happy' when I get that new china cabinet." We promise ourselves, "I'll be 'happy' when I get that new car or when I live in that subdivision." If my mate would just act like Ken or Barbie I know "I'll be 'happy' then." If the pastor would run the church right, if the boss knew how to manage better, and if they would just give me a new computer at work, "I'll be 'happy' then." No you won't. Happiness that is dependent on someone else's actions or on the purchase of stuff is not real happiness, and chasing happiness there shows you haven't reached true contentment. Most of us have acted like Steve Martin did in the movie *The Jerk*. In the movie, as he leaves his house in the middle of foreclosure, he says, "It doesn't matter, I don't need much to be happy, just this lamp, and this chair, and this . . . and this . . ." By the time he gets to the street he is covered with the items that are all it takes for him to be "happy."

STUDY THE SIGNS TO FIND YOUR WAY

At the root of the signs of discontentment is the answer to where contentment lies. The root of get-rich-quick thinking gives us a glimpse of our problem if we have this sign of discontentment in our life. I suffered from this type of impatience and still have to fight it back to this day. If you or your mate has always got an eye open for the next sure-fire moneymaking idea, I challenge you to sit down and spend some time thinking about contentment and its real sources. The heart of someone, including me, who thinks get-rich-quick schemes will work for them is the heart of a cheater. We think we are too bright, too pretty, or too good to have to take the "normal" path to wealth building. We "just know" that we have something special that exempts us from having to read the whole book and that allows us to just read the *Cliffs Notes*. Shortcuts just don't pay, but get-rich-quick hearts have an arrogance about them that is more than confidence. The other folks who fall in get-rich-quick sand are the desperate ones. Desperation gives you the heart of a cheater. If we are desperate enough, sometimes we think shortcuts are OK.

WHY DO THE FAITHFUL GET BLESSINGS?

The Bible says in Proverbs 28:20, "A faithful man will abound with blessings, But he who hastens to be rich will not go unpunished." Why do get-rich-quick folks always get punished and faithful people abound in blessings? Is God this big umpire that punishes you for shortcuts because you tried to cheat? No, the reason the get-rich-quick folks are punished, usually by losing their riches, is because character is more important than circumstances in the scope of eternity. Get-rich-quick folks still need to mold their value system into one that can truly find happiness. They are looking for love in all the wrong places, so the punishment is not for the offense of trying to get rich quick; the punishment is a course correction so that we learn to look for contentment and happiness where it can really be found. Faithful people are blessed the same way the tortoise wins the race because circumstances didn't decide for them how they were going to react; the character, the value system, that made them faithful didn't need molding. Contentment is found in character, not circumstances that are made better with money.

People who suffer from the need to appear rich quick can also give us a clue as to where to find contentment if we look at the core problem in their character. When we suffer from the need to appear wealthy we are suffering from a deep need for acceptance. We all suffer from a little of this disease because we all want to be loved; but to the level we let this need to appear rich make our financial

242 I **MORE THAN ENOUGH**

and relationship decisions we will crash and burn. We buy
things we can't afford and by the time we are through paying for it we hate the item. Proverbs 10:22 says, "The
blessing of the Lord makes one rich, And He adds not sorrow with it." If you have an item that has sorrow added to
it then it must not have been the Lord's blessing.

If an extreme need to please is at the core of this kind
of discontentment then it is easy to understand one of the
key steps to contentment. That key step is that you can
only be content to the extent that you are not motivated by
other people's shallow opinion of your actions or financial
decisions.

AMERICANS LOVE THEIR CARS

In America you are what you drive. We place more prestige on what you drive than virtually any purchase we
make. If you are rich then you must have a nice new car,
right? Actually that is wrong; most people who have built
wealth drive older reliable cars. In his study of millionaires, Thomas J. Stanley found that large homes and nice
new cars were not an indicator of a large portfolio; instead
they were actually an indicator of a lack of wealth. Too
many people have built a financial life that looks like a
movie set at Universal studios. The movie set for the sub-
urban street has beautiful large homes all down the street,
but of course you and I know what happens when you
walk through the front door—there is nothing. All show

and no substance seems to be some folks' motto. In order to have deep, abiding contentment in your financial and relationship decisions, you have to reach the point you just don't care what "people" think. I drive a ten-year-old car with over 150,000 miles on it and I keep it in near perfect condition. When you have gone broke like Sharon and I did over ten years ago, sorry, but we just don't care what you think anymore.

THIS IS A NO-WHINING ZONE

One morning, my pastor told a story to a group at my office that illustrates how far we have fallen in our need to impress and in our need to keep up. During the depression he lived in the rural South. His parents, like many people, felt blessed if they could just find work. They were both blessed with a job at the local factory six miles from their home, but they had no car. The neighbor down the road had a car, but Mom and Dad didn't have enough money to pay for gas for both to ride; so only one could. Mom rode in the car pool and Dad walked the six miles to work. Mom would of course get home much earlier than Dad and begin cooking dinner. My pastor recalled that about the time Mom would have dinner ready Dad would appear over the top of the last hill. Dad would come into the house with dust or snow to his knees from the six-mile hike; he would wash and sit down to eat. Each night they thanked God for the blessings of honest work. My pastor said he never once heard them whine about the circumstances. Where have *those* men gone?

Several years ago I met with a doctor and his wife about their finances. They were making $330,000 per year and had a household budget, including gardeners and maids, of over $368,000. When I tried to explain to this woman that her gardener would retire better off than she would and that she would have to cut some things out of their lifestyle she became very angry. This spoiled grown woman who was spending $38,000 per year more than they made began to whine about losing luxuries as if her life depended on them. Many of the people I meet with whine about everything. "You mean my children can't attend private school?" "You mean my children should share a bedroom?" "You mean we should try to exist with our second car being an old one so we have the money to save for retirement?" Concepts of short-term pain in order to have long-term gain can really bring out some world-class whining. Don't get me wrong, I don't want to walk six miles to work; but where have *those* men gone? Those were people of deep character who understood that not having everything wasn't the end of the world. If we want to have MORE THAN ENOUGH we need a strong dose of that depth of character.

IF YOU DESERVE TO BE HAPPY
YOU HAVE TO KNOW WHERE TO LOOK

I spent some time on the phone the other day with a friend who is thinking of ending his marriage. His statement was a standard statement for someone in a midlife crisis, "I just can't be happy with her and I deserve to be happy." You know how it always happens; you think of what you should have said fifteen minutes after you hang up. What I realized is my friend is depending on his mate's behavior for his happiness and contentment. That is seriously shallow and won't work. So in his effort to fix all his problems by "finding himself" in a red convertible with the secretary and joining a rock band, he will find himself cold, shivering, standing in the middle of the street wondering what happened. If you are miserable with $10 in the bank, you will be miserable with $1 million in mutual funds. If you don't have contentment in your current home you won't find it waiting in the spare bedroom of the larger one you thought would "make you happy." If you want to avoid the conflict of building your current marriage into a great one, you are going to be sadly disappointed if you switch to a newer model of mate, because ALL relationships involve some level of conflict. Whether it's friends, mates, or children, the deeper the relationship, the more conflict you have survived and grown through together.

Hate is not the opposite of love, apathy is. Hate actually creates almost the same reactions in your body that love does. The same chemicals like protein, adrenaline, and endorphins are released and the same kinds of changes in blood pressure, heart rate, perspiration, and eye dilation occur as a result of hate as love. You do not find contentment from circumstances or changing your circumstances. You find it by learning from your situation and fighting through it to make your character change and learning to win wherever you are.

CONTENTMENT IS BOTH THE FRUIT AND THE TREE

Contentment is both a cause and an effect; it is both a fruit and a tree that bears fruit. The fruit it bears is the peace and happiness that leads to stronger relationships and the ability to get out of debt, invest, and give. It is a fruit because contentment is not something you just sit down one morning and decide you will have that day. You can't hold your breathe until contentment comes, you will just turn blue and pass out. It is a mistake to accept what some gurus of supposed spirituality teach: that contentment is a state of being that you will into existence with positive affirmations or other methods. You can look in the mirror and say, "I am content, I am content" over and over, and when you realize it didn't work you will be more discontented. Contentment grows from your character. If you want to be more content and get the great benefits you have to go all the way back to chapter 1. You need to establish the proven keys in your life, in order, so that they build on one another; and by the time you get to this chapter, contentment will be the natural fruit of your character to the extent that you have established the keys.

We have to realize that contentment and happiness depend on character, not circumstances. We cannot always control the situations and circumstances of life. Life happens, but we can decide our attitude and responses before the situations arise. Those with poor self-esteem, a lack of values, and no vision continue to change jobs, cities, churches, and spouses in a desperate hunt for contentment and happiness. Talk about looking for love in all the wrong places.

MONEY CAN BUY FUN, BUT NOT HAPPINESS

There is nothing wrong with wanting a great relationship with your mate. There is nothing wrong with desiring to own some nice stuff. There is nothing wrong with going on nice vacations or indulging yourself occasionally. All of those things are fun. The problem comes when we confuse happiness and fun. You can buy fun. You can buy a fun vacation, but you have to come home. You can buy nice stuff, but it will grow old—and if it is a computer it is out of date by the time you get it plugged in. It is fun to watch your wife's eyes when you give her a big diamond, but by morning you still better pick up your underwear off of the bathroom floor. Happiness is about things that are real and that last. Happiness is when I say good-night prayers and one of my girls says, "Daddy, I love you." Happiness is a Sunday afternoon nap in my debt-free hammock. Happiness is decades of a growing and nurturing marriage. Happiness is investing your life to help others. The very sad truth is most people today don't see that anymore because they have gotten happiness and fun confused. They were helped by the disturbances created by marketing, and that lack of contentment actually ended up robbing them of the very thing they sought.

Contentment can be gathered again when we learn to slow down and count life's simple pleasures. We remember the old saying, "The happiest people don't necessarily *have* the best of everything, they *make* the best of everything." Contentment comes when we develop an attitude of gratitude for the important things we do have in our lives that we tend to take for granted if we have our eyes staring longingly at our neighbor's stuff.

HOW TO STOP WORRYING

As I said earlier, to the extent worry is with you, contentment can't be. Dale Carnegie said, "Eighty percent of the things people worry about never happen." Mr. Carnegie also taught how to manage worry and fear so that we can reach toward contentment. He said to divide your worries into two groups: worries you can do something about, and the ones you can't. The worries you can't do anything about like "the economy" or "nuclear war" you need to let go of, because it is a waste of brainpower and emotional energy to worry about something over which you have absolutely no control. The worries you can do something about like family problems, career scares, and money being short are the ones you should spend your brainpower and energy doing something about. Instead of worrying, harness all the energy into creating a plan that you can implement to solve the problem, ease your worry, and arrive at contentment. I have watched hundreds of families have tremendous contentment and peace while losing jobs or having huge financial problems. How did they do it? They had worked, planned, thought about everything they could do, and they had done it. They got great peace knowing that they had done all they could. They recognized that the rest of the mess will just fall where it will, but because they had been diligent in their preparation they could be at peace about having taken responsibility for circumstances and having done the very best they could within their means— financially and spiritually. Art Williams says, "All you can do is all you can do, and that is enough."

I read once that happiness is not a state to arrive at, it is a manner of the traveling. I believe one key to contentment is to really understand that. In Luke 12:15 Jesus said, ". . . for one's life does not consist in the abundance of the things he possesses." You truly have to learn to count your blessings; to make a list of the great things in your life; and to place value on people, relationships, and the things that you own.

THE CONTENTMENT CATAPULT

The fun thing is that when you start to hit some new levels of contentment and peace you will be catapulted into yet even higher levels. These new levels of contentment come because you make better long-term financial and relationship decisions when you are content. Since you become wealthier and have better relationships you will become more content, so contentment really does lead you to more contentment.

Larry and Eva live the lives of the real millionaires; They drive older cars, live in a middle-class house, and invest compulsively. They were able to build wealth quickly because no matter how much money they had, they never raised their lifestyle and always invested the increases in their income. By the time they were in their forties they already had created a net worth of $2 million. Their level of contentment and feelings of security enabled them to make a very risky $200,000 investment in a high-tech start-up computer company that, you guessed it, ended up exploding in growth. Their $200,000 investment became worth another $3 million. They were secure and content before the wealth, but their contentment led first to a $2 million net worth, and then to a $5 million net worth. That's the power of contentment!

And your newfound peace and the actions it creates will begin to rub off on your closest family and friends. You can't help but impact them with the different decisions you make and the example you set for those around you. But first, you have to achieve contentment of your own. You need to begin by taking a good hard look at what you have and what you think you want. As you think about these questions, try making a list of your blessings and your worries. Use the joy and peace you receive from your blessings to give you the energy and motivation to tackle your worries. Use journaling to give yourself perspective on where you are and how to find contentment from the place you are now: from your relationships, your children, your work, your home, your friends, and from your community. Work through your impatience, work through your envy, work toward contentment and peace.

A HUNDRED DOLLARS WILL BUY A LOT

My middle child Rachel brought home a project from kindergarten several years ago that really shows this to be true. The kindergarten teacher had the kids draw a picture and write under it what they would do if they had $100—to them somewhere close to $10 million. The teacher then took these drawings and made a little book called "If I Had a Hundred Dollars." The book was then sent home to the parents to enjoy with all the other kindergarten projects. Sharon and I were sitting on the floor of the den in front of the couch looking through the kids' papers for the week when we discovered this treasure.

You must understand that Rachel is our most dramatic child and the one we have to watch the closest because she has such a zest for life. Sometimes that zest is called strong-willed. She was also born the year we filed bankruptcy and started over after losing everything. We started over with a strange new peace that comes from having your soul cleansed by a very hot fire. Because of what happened the year Rachel was born we worry little, we don't have a need to get or appear rich quick, and we definitely don't envy others like we used to. These changes in our character are all that Rachel has ever observed; she wasn't born when we were motivated by our discontentment into some really stupid decisions. Rachel has only watched our new life, so she is our little barometer of these keys to MORE THAN ENOUGH.

So as we opened the book, we didn't know what to expect. As Sharon and I looked at what these kids wanted to buy we were tickled by how their desires were a mirror of our culture. Scott H. said he wanted "a car that changes into everything" and Anna K. said she wanted "a house with a cat." We kept turning pages. Andrew wanted "a football, a swimming pool, a gun, and a bomb"; I guess he was a small terrorist. Sue said if she had $100 she would "buy a swimming pool with a whale like Free Willie." Then we got to Rachel's page wondering what kind of wildness we would find. We were caught off guard when we read her words: "If I had $100 I would give it to the poor people."

That kind of beautiful statement is born of contentment, not of an "I'll be happy when" heart. That kind of heart will know the true happiness that only comes from helping others while the next-door neighbor gets a new pool or leases yet another car and feels a gnawing emptiness. Real contentment is born in the spiritual. And each day as I close my national radio show, I say, "There is ultimately only one way to financial peace, and that is to walk daily with the Prince of Peace, Christ Jesus."

THE STORY CONTINUES

Out of core *values, vision* is born. *Vision* is put into work clothes and becomes *goals.* Shared *goals* give you *unity* with those who are on the journey with you. *Values, vision,* and *unity* repair broken *hope* and build *hope* into the fuel that fires the rocket of *intensity.* The rocket of *intensity* is kept between the ditches by *accountability* and *support.* The pilot of the rocket ensuring that *intensity* stays on *vision's* course is *diligence.* His copilot and navigator are *work* and *discipline. Patience* that is born of power has at its center *intensity, hope, vision,* and *diligence.* You can't have real *patience* without first having those things and when you have it relationships are built and you add yet more *unity. Contentment* is the fruit of all of these. *Contentment* is born way back at *values,* is nurtured by *vision* and *unity,* is given a cool drink by *hope,* and is fed by *accountability* and *support. Contentment* then becomes the tree that bears a higher quality of *values, vision, hope, diligence, patience,* and a quiet *intensity.*

Thoughts from Sharon . . .

In order for you to be content with your lifestyle, you need to be content with your life. For a lot of people that is a very difficult thing to do. Some people can seem to have very little and still be content. You have to be thankful for what you have because if you think about it, it could be a lot worse. There are probably people out there who would trade places with you in a second.

The story of "I'll be happy when I get . . ." has lived and played a part in everyone's lives. Hey, we have all said it, I definitely know I have. What David says about the china cabinet is true, because I knew I'd be happy when I had one!

After going broke once and knowing we didn't want to go there again, it made me realize what real contentment was all about. I did not always feel content during those years, but I realized that life was supposed to be fun. So I had to learn to live one day at a time and be thankful for what I did have and not worry about the things that we didn't have or that we had lost. I had a home to live in, I had a healthy husband and children, and I had food on the table. I still have that and more and I'm very thankful for everything the Lord has provided. Contentment is more than things, or stuff; it's your ability to cope with and deal with your situation and circumstances. We did it, you can too.

Keys to the More Than Enough Mansion

1. Change is very hard and we change only when the pain of *same* is greater than the pain of change.
2. Cleansing cries and hinge pins are signals that we are ready.
3. Values really do matter and real values are the foundation of everything to come.
4. Integrity—real deep integrity, even with the little things—is vital because deception destroys.
5. Connectedness is key; take time to use the sidewalks that connect you to family, friends, and coworkers.
6. Vision that is rooted in values is the only vision that will last.
7. Vision makes you a long-term investor, not living for the moment.
8. Goals are the building blocks of vision, vision in work clothes.
9. Model for and teach your children about vision and goals.
10. Opposites attract and men and women are different; identify and admit those differences and use each other's strengths for MORE THAN ENOUGH.
11. Men, build an emergency fund and leave it alone; it will change the way your wife treats you.
12. Budgeting together brings tremendous oneness

to your marriage, but you must die to selfishness; the "you" in "unity" must be silent.

13. Hope is lost when it is placed in people, stuff, and institutions.

14. Hope is lost when we believe failure is permanent and we lose perspective.

15. Hope is an act of the will and moves people to action.

16. Return to strong values and the vision born of them to rekindle your hope.

17. Small groups for support and encouragement are the most powerful form of behavior modification known.

18. When holding your spouse accountable use "I feel" statements that aren't so threatening.

19. Pride busting and encouragement when needed are the lost art of the mentor.

20. To reach **MORE THAN ENOUGH** you have to be as intense as the gazelle is when running from the cheetah: gazelle intensity.

21. Gazelle intensity given focus will create momentum; and momentum in relationships and wealth building brings almost inexplicable illogical things into your life.

22. Work is doing it, discipline is doing it every day, and diligence is doing it well every day.

23. No one has **MORE THAN ENOUGH** in relationships or

wealth without hard work, discipline, and diligence.

24. Patience is golden and like gold is purified in the fires of life.

25. Patience brings real power to your wealth building and a real quality to your relationships because you are looking long term.

26. Patience makes you an investor who stays in the market and reaps long-term rewards, and patience demands you save to pay cash so you avoid debt.

27. Contentment is possibly the most powerful financial principle; with it, getting out of debt, saving, and giving are easy.

28. Watch for the thieves of contentment: the extreme level of marketing in our culture that makes us want more, envy, and get-rich-quick and appear-rich quick schemes.

29. You won't be happy when. . . . Happiness is a decision to be content where you are now; don't confuse fun and happiness.

11

The Great Misunderstanding

A few weeks ago Toni came to visit me. Toni and her husband Jerry had some very hard times about eight years ago and I had counseled them through the mess. As a newlywed couple they had bought everything they "needed" to be "happy," from expensive jewelry to electronics to a car they couldn't afford. If you think hard enough you probably know this couple. After buying all this stuff, of course, Jerry lost his job and they got behind in their bills and were facing bankruptcy. It took several years, but they made it out of the hole and are prospering now. During our visit, Toni reminded me of something that happened eight years ago that turned them around. When they had come to meet me that afternoon, they were in full-pity party mode. Life was bad, unfair, and "how could anyone be expected to live through all the bad stuff that was happening to them." They had a new baby and were worried where the diaper money was going to come from. Honestly, I was a little tired and wasn't really compassionate with their whining, but I listened for about an hour and made some adjustments to their budgets and talked about the job hunt. It was time for them to leave when my phone rang. Our church was on the line and needed someone to take some food to a lady in the subsidized housing project. I didn't have time that day to do it myself, but then a light bulb came on: "Why not send Mr. and Mrs. Whiner?" They would most likely spend the next several hours sucking their thumbs so maybe they would feel better if they had something to do. I had no idea as I sent them out the door to get the church's money and to deliver some food how important an assignment it would turn out to be.

They picked up the church's money and a list of what the lady needed and headed toward the grocery store. When they saw all the items she needed as compared to the amount the church had given them, they were sure there was no way. Toni and Jerry had a huge fight in the grocery store because Jerry was determined to get everything and kept shopping and putting things back until he made it work. Toni said they were so mad they were throwing things into the buggy. Finally, with the entire list of items bought, they headed for the lady's apartment. When they got there they found horrible conditions and a lady without hope. She was in her early thirties; her husband had been murdered in another city and she had traveled to our city with her toddler to find work, to try to start over. She had no food left, no job, and no mate, living in a dirty apartment, and to top it all off her baby had just been diagnosed with terminal leukemia. The dying toddler was about the same age as Toni and Jerry's healthy baby. To Toni and Jerry's credit they spent the afternoon with this lady helping her by showing her how to save and do a budget the way I had taught them. They encouraged her, and they prayed with her.

Toni said as she and Jerry drove away from that lady's apartment they looked at each other and both began to cry, feeling very ashamed for their pity party earlier in the afternoon. Toni told me that their act of giving up their afternoon to deliver groceries to someone with real need changed their lives. That day something broke loose inside them and their finances and relationship began to improve. That day they were lifted out of their problems by giving.

HOLD ON LOOSE

Golda Meir said, "You can't shake hands with a clenched fist." The fist is the international sign of anger or of a closed spirit. Even a dog understands an open hand and will come wagging his tail, but the fist makes his approach skittish. The open hand is a gesture of invitation and acceptance. That gesture of acceptance can come most easily to someone who is not scared himself. When we are scared we fight, clench our fists, and prepare for battle because we don't have the perception or position of strength to avoid a fight. So while the closed fist is a sign of battle, it is born of weakness.

I see the closed fist often in the area of money: a fist full of dollars tightly held so that those precious dollars never get away. That closed fist represents someone who doesn't know how to give. They think if they clutch those dollars tight enough, never giving, that they are on the path to **MORE THAN ENOUGH**. The real world will teach you that the opposite is true; those with **MORE THAN ENOUGH** got there by giving. The clenched money fist, just like the anger fist, is born of weakness. People who don't give do so because of their pitiful shortsighted misunderstanding of how money really works. These folks are so weak and insecure that they honestly believe they will have more by hoarding and gripping those dollars.

The problem with holding money with an open hand is that it violates common sense. We feel that if we don't tightly hold on to our money and our relationships, then they will slip away. If you hold ten $100 bills ($1,000) with your palm open the wind may carry the money away or someone could easily snatch your hard-earned money from you. How could that be smart? And the truth is simply letting your money blow away or be taken from you isn't smart. The open hand comes in when we talk about our attitude toward money. The open hand represents how you must hold money and relationships in your emotions and spirit if you want **MORE THAN ENOUGH**. The people who are the happiest and the wealthiest got that way by giving. If we clench those dollars so tightly that they won't leave, they won't.

The great misunderstanding is that holding on to

your money gives the result you want; the problem with the clenched-fist money-management style is that while those dollars can't get away, new dollars can't get in either. You can't add dollars because you are holding the ones you have so tightly. The only way to add dollars is to open the hand and that is representative of giving. When you give you open yourself up; you allow the dollars the freedom to leave, and the freedom to enter.

MATURITY SHOWS UP AGAIN

A few years back, I was serving on the board of a nonprofit organization that was in the middle of a fund-raising campaign. We hired a group to help us raise money, which presented us with a study on giving patterns that shocked us and explained a lot. The study was a survey of over 100,000 people of all ages; one of the most revealing things it showed was the difference in how various age groups view giving. The study asked people to describe "their most memorable giving experience." People over sixty described a lifetime of monthly giving as "their most memorable giving experience." They received the best return from a lifetime of steady giving. People thirty to sixty years old explained the one time they helped someone in a dramatic way: the time the tornado hit and they donated time and money or the time the missionary was at the church with pictures that made them cry so they gave. They apparently didn't have the lifetime of steady giving to look at as an option. The most shocking response was from the under-thirty crowd. When asked to describe "their most memorable giving experience" the folks under thirty described *receiving* something! They recalled Dad giving them a car when they turned sixteen or that Christmas when Santa brought the new bike that they wanted so badly. I do not think that younger people are more selfish than older folks are. I do believe that there are many people under sixty who give every week or month to their church or other valid places to give. However, this study shows us two things overall. First, the more mature we are the more we realize how stupid it is to think that by holding tightly and never giving we will achieve **MORE THAN ENOUGH**. Second, this study shows us the impact of marketing and how it makes us more selfish. The under-thirty crowd has been hit with two to three times more marketing than the over-sixty crowd because of the under-thirty crowd's obsession with media, TV, radio, the Web, etc. Holding on at all cost shows weakness, selfishness, and a lack of maturity. Giving shows strength, perspective, maturity, and a noble selflessness that has become rare.

I was talking about giving as a part of a healthy financial plan on my radio show one day and a guy called in and very bitterly showed how clenched his fist was. He said, "I give to starving children—mine." Funny line, but he meant it. He really believes the best way for him and his family to have **MORE THAN ENOUGH** is the clenched-fist approach and it just won't work.

Sadly, many of us feel the same way this man does. The

group Empty Tomb did a study of evangelical churches, which shows that giving as a percentage of income went up during the Great Depression and down during World War II (folks were giving to the war effort, not their church). The other conclusion of the study was that church giving as a percentage of income is at an all time low since 1921 (except World War II). The average church attendees give only 2.39 percent of their income when the biblical standard is 10 percent. The Christian giving scandals of the eighties can take partial blame for this, but more than anything the lack of church giving is representative of what our culture has been teaching us over the last forty years. We have been misled into believing that the way to MORE THAN ENOUGH is the clenched fist, never letting those dollars go for fear we won't have enough. Remember it is only the open hand that will allow dollars in. The really sad thing about this 2.39 percent giving is that while these folks think they are keeping dollars they are losing them and the other benefits of giving.

GIVING TO GET DOESN'T WORK

Some of you have gotten the wrong message by now. You are thinking that I am saying you should give because it is a guaranteed formula to get—wrong. If you give because you think that makes God owe you a favor and you are promised to get more, you will mess up the whole process. When you give expecting, you are selfish, and that does not bring you more money or better relationships. When you give expecting nothing in return is when **More Than Enough** will visit you every time. That is when joy visits you and your chin is lifted, vision is increased, and your quality of life is peaked yet again and again.

Why does giving work in the formula for **More Than Enough**? Giving works because you are designed to be a giving being. Your wiring schematic is built for giving. You are made in God's image and He is a giver; so that means in order for you to be all you can be you must be a giver too. Your emotions, spirit, psyche, and even your chemistry are changed to a higher level when you give. When you give, creativity is enhanced—ask Michelangelo about the Sistine Chapel. When you give, passion, joy, and intensity come to you like waves crashing at the seashore. When you give you move along the selfishness line toward unselfishness, and that causes relationships to be better or even healed. After one of my day-long financial seminars, a pastor approached me to give me an example of how giving affects relationships. He said that in thirty-five years of ministering a large congregation he had never had a couple file for divorce who gave their Christian tenth of their income.

When you give you are getting maximum horsepower out of your personal design. People who don't give are stopped up. Things flow in but nothing flows out. We all know that anything that is stopped up eventually begins to stink. What happens to the pond on the farm that water flows into, but not out of? It grows something on the surface of the water, scum. People who don't give get scummy. You have felt the scumminess of them when you meet with them; their greed, selfishness, arrogance, and fear are warping their decisions so that they see you only as a business unit, instead of a long-term relationship. I have acquaintances who are always getting into some new group to get rich and are calling to include me in the best deal since sliced bread. I always feel like a unit when I meet with them; I feel like I have walked through a spider web that got all over me as I tried to pick the greed and selfishness off of me after the meeting.

SOWING AND REAPING

Giving works because it is your personal blueprint to be a giver, and you unleash good things in your life that you will never see until you learn the art of unselfish giving. Earl Nightingale talks about the power of sowing and reaping in the classic motivational recording *The Strangest Secret.* Nightingale says that we reap what we sow; you have probably heard that before, but how you apply that concept shows your level of understanding. You are planting seeds when you give and when you don't give. If you plant nothing, by default you planted weeds. If you plant nightshade, a deadly poison, the ground will provide you a great crop of poison. If you plant corn, don't scratch your head and wonder why you got corn. The earth and life will return to you what you plant in great abundance. The sad thing is that most people don't plant and are real confused as to why they get a great crop of weeds, a great crop of being average. You must plant on purpose what you want if you want **MORE THAN ENOUGH**. Become a farmer for life, till the field, and the well-plowed field is ready to grow things.

Matthew is a man who definitely has **MORE THAN ENOUGH**. When he and his wife Beverly were first married, she came to him about their giving. Beverly suggested they raise their regular support of a nonprofit group they were involved in. They did that faithfully and every year for the next six years Matthew's income doubled. His income doubled because he is very bright and a very hard worker, but also because when you give you unleash powerful things in your life.

GIVING GIVES YOU UNDERSTANDING

Giving is an amazing process because it violates common sense, which tells us if we let go we will have less not more. Giving, though, lifts us out of ourselves; we take our eyes off our rights, our problems, and our stuff. That new view gives us renewed vision and hope. Giving is powerful.

Eight years ago I started giving advice differently to financially troubled couples partly because of what I witnessed in Toni and Jerry. If you are struggling in your relationship or your wallet a very productive thing to do is give. Maybe you don't have money, but go to your local homeless shelter and serve soup. Then sit at the table and eat some of the soup with the men and women you have served it to. Take your mate and your kids with you; it will do the family good to reset their view of reality. Go to a nursing home and read to the elderly for an afternoon. Help someone change a tire. Spend some time helping or teaching those in prison. It is easy to find people with real problems when you simply look. When you give of yourself you can't help but be lifted up and energized to fight your own problems. Your own problems are easier to fight through when you realize how small they really are in comparison to what some of your fellowmen face.

WE GET CONFUSED MESSAGES

Our Dr. Jekyll and Mr. Hyde culture gives us one message and then turns on us. We are taught that becoming wealthy is the peak of success. Everything is measured in wealth. Go for it! Grab all you can! If you just gather enough stuff, you will not only be happy, you will also "be somebody"! Our culture pushes us to build wealth, to gather stuff and power, then our culture turns on us and blames all the problems of the world on "rich" people. The have-nots are always blaming every evil out there on the haves. If you are a have-not "you must be lazy or dumb," but then when you work your fingers to the bone and build wealth some bonehead is always around to act like everything is your fault. "All those rich people don't really care about anything but money; they should give it all away to help the poor." "If that person was a real spiritual person how can he hoard all that money for himself." I hear pitiful shallow statements or hints of that way of looking at things running all through the media, our politics, and our culture.

We used to be a country that admired diligence, thrift, and integrity. What we must remember is that money allows us the leverage to do good. If you want to truly have **MORE THAN ENOUGH** you have to understand that the reason for building wealth is first to give you and your family security and second to see how many people you can help. When many folks talk about the wealthy giving they don't understand how proper giving should be done. Proper giving is understanding that we don't give away everything and start over because when we do we lose the power to help. The weak can't lift what the strong can. If you pull your muscles by overlifting you lose your ability to lift at all. Margaret Thatcher said, "No one would remember the Good Samaritan if he only had good intentions. He had money as well." Money is to serve you and those you help; it is not for you to serve. P. T. Barnum stated it well when he said, "Money is a terrible master, but an excellent servant." If you want to be a powerful giver you should view your wealth as the goose and give the golden eggs. If you give away the goose, the golden eggs are gone and so is your ability to help others. Those of you who think "those nasty rich people should be made to give up the wealth they have earned" are not only stupid; your short-sightedness kills the goose, and the poor are not really helped. The habits, character traits, and abilities that make someone able to build wealth also make him able to manage it. Yes, there are rich jerks with low morals and the inability to give and help others, but I can promise you that they are the minority.

Many of the wealthy understand it is not a privilege, but instead a great responsibility to have wealth. One of the wealthiest men in the world in the early 1900s, Andrew Carnegie, understood this responsibility when he said, "Surplus wealth is a sacred trust which its possessor is bound to administer in his lifetime for the good of the community." Andrew Carnegie not only talked about giving; he did it. Of course you have heard of Carnegie Hall, and the Carnegie fortune is responsible for the starting of and much of the growth of the public library system nationwide. Carnegie believed in libraries because when he was a very young man following the Civil War many of the country's books had been destroyed. A Civil War veteran colonel allowed young Carnegie and a few other young men access to his extensive and private library. Carnegie often credited his huge success to the lessons learned in those pages.

IT IS EASIER IF YOU DON'T "OWN" IT

I used to own a real estate company that managed property for landlords. We collected rents, paid the bills, and sent the owner the profits. If the heating and air unit broke down, fixing it meant spending someone else's money, so we may have felt bad but we certainly didn't lie awake in paralyzed worry. When you view wealth with an open hand rather than a closed fist you behave as we did at my real estate company. The understanding that the wealth is really God's and you are managing it not only for yourself, but also for the good of others frees you. People who emotionally and spiritually hold their wealth with an open hand don't feel an ownership of their stuff. If you release the ownership emotionally, then you have a better view of what should be done with the money you manage. This release of emotional ownership is called generosity. The folks who are able to emotionally release the ownership of stuff and feel more like managers don't worry as much. Antoine Rivaroli said, "There are men who gain from their wealth only the fear of losing it." If you release ownership emotionally you don't worry, because while you want to manage as well as you can, you don't have a white-knuckle grip on those dollars that always have worry tied to them.

Have you ever met an arrogant rich person? I have; as a matter of fact, I've met several. The arrogance, the ego trip, comes from them somehow getting the idea that they are actually worth what they have. They have emotional ownership, a closed fist. The same release of ownership we were talking about virtually guarantees that as you build wealth you won't become arrogant. It is very hard to be arrogant about something you manage for someone else. Remember that is the emotional position those who have MORE THAN ENOUGH put themselves in.

THE PATH TO TRUE JOY

The great misunderstanding that holding instead of releasing makes us happy, that being served instead of serving makes us happy, and that mere possession of wealth
will make us happy steals our very being from us. The happiest and most joyful people are those who give money
and serve. It seems contrary to everything our culture
screams at us, but look at the culture's track record: teen
suicide, a record high for bankruptcies and divorces, kids
killing kids in the schoolhouse. We aren't very happy. True
joy comes from serving. Bill Hybels's book, *Descending
into Greatness*, does a beautiful job of defeating the myth
that greatness and joy are found by ascending. We serve
and give our way into true joy. That is not some false religious statement made up to fill pages in a chapter.

Think of the times you have been happiest. I'll bet, if
you aren't thinking of fun but deep contentment and happiness, you are thinking of a time you poured yourself into
someone or some cause that was of no direct benefit to
you. Serving, helping others really does make you have
MORE THAN ENOUGH. Room mothers at the elementary
school, Girl Scout leaders, Little League coaches, missionaries, Boy Scout leaders, and volunteers of all kinds
know that while sometimes helping others can be frustrating, it is always rewarding and brings joy. A Boy Scout
leader shared one of his mottoes with me: "A hundred
years from now it will not matter what my bank account
was, the sort of house I lived in, or the kind of car I drove.

But the world may be different, because I was important in the life of a boy." Helen Keller said, "Life is an exciting business, and most exciting when it is lived for others."

MY, THIS IS NOBLE

Many of you have decided by now that I am calling you to a higher level of nobility and I am. But sometimes you just don't fell like giving or serving, sometimes you feel like a sponge with all the water rung out. I am calling you higher, but also from a very practical viewpoint. If you aren't happy, serve and give more. Yes, you can almost approach giving and serving from the selfish view that you want the happiness they will send. "Life is a place of service," Leo Tolstoy said, "joy can be real only if people look upon their life as a service and have a definite object in life outside themselves and their personal happiness." The great leaders, thinkers, and some of the most noble among us have a lot to say on the subject of giving to receive true joy. At the end of their lives if you could have visited their bedsides they would not have told you of regrets from giving, but of lives filled with meaning and happiness. Albert Schweitzer said, "I don't know what your destiny will be, but one thing I know; the only ones among you who will be really happy are those who will have sought and found how to serve."

So as you and I continue to uncover the proven keys to **MORE THAN ENOUGH** you must understand the great misunderstanding. You have MORE THAN ENOUGH only when you give it away. Give of yourself, of your time, and view your wealth as being managed for others. John Wesley, the great evangelist and founder of the Methodist Church, said, "Do all the good you can to all the people you can, in all the ways you can, as long as you ever can."

YOU NEVER KNOW HOW IT IS GOING TO WORK

Several years ago, Ed and Lucy sat with me and I taught them the importance of giving as they were digging out of a financial mess. They had about $12,000 in credit card debt, had a house they couldn't afford, but they believed me on the subject of giving. They began to give to their church every week. Three months later Ed was diagnosed with cancer. I remember visiting him in the hospital. With a death sentence from the doctors he was poking fun at me, saying, "Wow, look what your giving got me." He was being sarcastic because even in the middle of that mess, Ed was at peace and happy. He had several very expensive operations to try to survive. I remember running into Ed and Lucy after he beat the cancer, and she ran over and told me that even though Ed hadn't worked in two years that they were actually in better financial shape after the cancer than before. His church and his work friends had raised money for his medical bills, and they had sold the house and were completely debt free. Cancer free and debt free, and I don't think in this life we can underestimate how big a role their giving played in both those results. Giving unleashes things we don't understand and can't explain.

THIS IS A TEST

Prosperity may be a bigger test than poverty when it comes to exposing your weaknesses. Fear, worry, selfishness, and arrogance are all some people get with wealth, but they are not MORE THAN ENOUGH people. People who get MORE THAN ENOUGH turn the great misunderstanding into the greatest understanding. They get a firm grip on the fact that a firm grip on the money is not the path to happiness and fulfillment. True prosperity is not wealth, it is MORE THAN ENOUGH, which can include wealth, but must include the loose holding of that wealth.

Finding ways to give shouldn't be hard. There are thousands and thousands of church, community, medical, and cultural groups in our society that need our help for them to be able to fulfill their missions. Find a group whose purpose you care about deeply and then donate your time, energy, and money to them. If you don't know where or how to give talk to your pastor or a leader in your community. Involve your spouse in the decision about where to give your money and share your voluntary efforts with your children. Take them along when you coach that inner-city softball team; have them tag along when you visit the elderly at the local nursing home; have them join you when you go read to a blind person. Sharing your efforts to give with your children will teach them, in turn, to be givers too. The rewards will grow exponentially: You will be helping others, deepening your relationships with your spouse and children, and opening your heart and fist in giving. As Bob Gass, a well-known evangelist, says, "Prosperity is having the money to do God's will in your life."

Giving and serving are truly the way to **MORE THAN ENOUGH.** Mentally, emotionally, financially, and spiritually balanced people have learned the value of making the great misunderstanding the greatest path to happiness and joy.

THE STORY CONTINUES

Out of core *values, vision* is born. *Vision* is put into work clothes and becomes *goals.* Shared *goals* give you *unity* with those who are on the journey with you. *Values, vision,* and *unity* repair broken *hope* and build *hope* into the fuel that fires the rocket of *intensity.* The rocket of *intensity* is kept between the ditches by *accountability* and *support.* The pilot of the rocket ensuring that *intensity* stays on *vision's* course is *diligence.* His copilot and navigator are *work* and *discipline. Patience* that is born of power has at its center *intensity, hope, vision,* and *diligence.* You can't have real *patience* without first having those things and when you have it relationships are built and you add yet more *unity. Contentment* changes your *vision,* gives you a different kind of *intensity,* definitely fuels *patience, diligence,* and *unity* while it is also born of all those things. *Giving* is the result of *values* and the *vision* they bring. *Unity* is increased by *giving* because relationships are affected. You always have more *hope* when pouring your life into something that matters. Part of the great misunderstanding is that somehow *giving* is the act of someone who isn't *intense* or *diligent* when in fact the opposite is true. *Patience* and *contentment* rise to a whole new level of understanding when they bring on *giving,* which then in turn feeds you more of each of those.

Thoughts from Sharon . . .

It seems that in our world today people need to learn again to give not just money, but also more of their time. Sometimes we get caught up in our lives and we lose sight of what's important. We need to be more caring for others.

We also need to teach these values to our children. Children learn from adults. When they see us helping and giving, they will also help and give. Here's a true example: This summer, the kids and I had been taking supper to an elderly couple who were Dave's neighbors when he was younger (she broke her hip and can't do much). This couple is so lonely. I can see the joy on their faces when we walk in to visit. They live for someone to come and knock on their door, and all we have to do is take the time.

I want my children to see this kind of love and hope they will have memories of this story. I want them to spread the joy of giving to others too.

Keys to the More Than Enough Mansion

1. Change is very hard and we change only when the pain of *same* is greater than the pain of change.
2. Cleansing cries and hinge pins are signals that we are ready.
3. Values really do matter and real values are the foundation of everything to come.

4. Integrity—real deep integrity, even with the little things—is vital because deception destroys.

5. Connectedness is key; take time to use the sidewalks that connect you to family, friends, and coworkers.

6. Vision that is rooted in values is the only vision that will last.

7. Vision makes you a long-term investor, not living for the moment.

8. Goals are the building blocks of vision, vision in work clothes.

9. Model for and teach your children about vision and goals.

10. Opposites attract and men and women are different; identify and admit those differences and use each other's strengths for MORE THAN ENOUGH.

11. Men, build an emergency fund and leave it alone; it will change the way your wife treats you.

12. Budgeting together brings tremendous oneness to your marriage, but you must die to selfishness; the "you" in "unity" must be silent.

13. Hope is lost when it is placed in people, stuff, and institutions.

14. Hope is lost when we believe failure is permanent and we lose perspective.

15. Hope is an act of the will and moves people to action.

16. Return to strong values and the vision born of them to rekindle your hope.

17. Small groups for support and encouragement are the most powerful form of behavior modification known.

18. When holding your spouse accountable use "I feel" statements that aren't so threatening.

19. Pride busting and encouragement when needed are the lost art of the mentor.

20. To reach MORE THAN ENOUGH you have to be as intense as the gazelle is when running from the cheetah: gazelle intensity.

21. Gazelle intensity given focus will create momentum, and momentum in relationships and wealth building brings almost inexplicable illogical things into your life.

22. Work is doing it, discipline is doing it every day, and diligence is doing it well every day.

23. No one has MORE THAN ENOUGH in relationships or wealth without hard work, discipline, and diligence.

24. Patience is golden and like gold is purified in the fires of life.

25. Patience brings real power to your wealth building and a real quality to your relationships because you are looking long term.

26. Patience makes you an investor who stays in the

market and reaps long-term rewards, and patience demands you save to pay cash so you avoid debt.

27. Contentment is possibly the most powerful financial principle; with it, getting out of debt, saving, and giving are easy.

28. Watch for the thieves of contentment: the extreme level of marketing in our culture that makes us want more, envy, and get-rich-quick and appear-rich-quick schemes.

29. You won't be happy when. . . . Happiness is a decision to be content where you are now; don't confuse fun and happiness.

30. The great misunderstanding is that we think we have to hoard to get, when in reality you can only have **MORE THAN ENOUGH** by releasing ownership spiritually and emotionally, then showing that by giving time and money away.

31. The most pure joy you will ever experience is to give your time and your money because you were designed to be a giver by God, you were made in His image.

12

The More Than Enough Road

As we have traveled together on the MORE THAN ENOUGH road, we have explored many different kinds of territory. We have looked at what makes us rich in spirit and in our pocketbooks. We have seen that getting rich quick in any arena doesn't work, because achieving MORE THAN ENOUGH is a process, a process that requires time and diligence. In an age when all our answers and information come in sound bites, we have lost an understanding of working through a process. And even more critically, we have lost the understanding of what true wisdom is. Since we have so much information at our fingertips, from encyclopedias on CD-ROMs to the Web to twenty-four-hour news and weather channels, we have learned to run our lives on summaries. We say, "I don't want all the data when making a business decision. I want the executive summary." The need to summarize and prioritize is healthy with our information overload, but the result is that we have lost the time it takes to deeply search out life-changing and life-forming wisdom. We have become creatures who exist on the surface who don't take the time to go deep—instead we go wide.

Wisdom, an ancient term, has been exchanged for mere cleverness or a cute quick comeback, the sound bite replacement to true wisdom. We sometimes think of intellect as being wisdom, but it ain't so. We all know people with great intellects who can't seem to function outside of a vacuum. Correct answers on a test are important, but that is not wisdom. Intellect, pure intelligence, is a wonderful thing, but when searching for the answers to the important questions of the MORE THAN ENOUGH life, intellect is no substitute for wisdom.

Who would you rather spend an evening with, someone very, very wealthy or someone very, very wise? Both might be intimidating to be around; but we all know most people would choose the wealthy person, because sadly in our culture we respect and admire wealth more than wisdom. We all know that wealth is not a way to tell for sure that someone is wise, but we have all made the mistake of thinking that wealth is more important than wisdom. Yes, you have too.

WISDOM DOES BUILD WEALTH

God asked Solomon what he desired and the answer was wisdom. Most scholars agree that Solomon was the wisest man to ever live and he became very wealthy. If he had desired wealth that might have been granted, but would not have given Solomon the MORE THAN ENOUGH way of life he had. Not all the wealthy are wise, but usually the wise will become wealthy given time. Wisdom almost always will lead to wealth because of the character traits that make up wisdom.

We tend to view wisdom as some little fat guru on a mountaintop, sitting there ready to answer all of life's questions like some ATM of knowledge. Wisdom is more than that and it usually comes with time, age, and experience. While we would all like to think of ourselves as respecters and pursuers of wisdom, we move in directions that prove the opposite. Our culture worships youth rather than age and the wisdom that goes with it. Too often, we view aging as something to dread and too many of us treat the "white head" as an incompetent person instead of seeing him as a source of wisdom. Proverbs 16:31 says, "The silver-haired head is the crown of glory, If it is found in the way of righteousness." You are more likely to find the wise among those who have experience than those who are just starting out. Wisdom comes from making mistakes, watching others make mistakes, and doing so over and over again until we begin to make the changes that are required not to make the same mistakes over again.

SOMETHING IN US MAKES
US REACH FOR THE STARS

Unless you are really stupid you would agree that it would be nice to have more wisdom, to have insight into matters and into what matters at a level you don't have now. If your hope is in place, you want to maximize more, optimize more, and reach deeper into the bucket of life. Stephen R. Covey says, "We want to Live, to Learn, and to Leave a Legacy." We all know that most of the time we don't use all that we have, that we aren't maximizing our potential to become greater than we are. Charlie Brown, the motivational speaker, says, "Life is like a ten-speed bicycle, most of us have gears we never use." Researchers have long told us that we use only about 10 percent of our brain's capacity.

American psychologist Abraham Maslow developed a model of human motivation known as Maslow's hierarchy of needs. The first level that humans tend to take care of before anything else is physiological needs, the basics like food, shelter, clothing, and transportation. When those needs are met we reach for level two: safety and security. That is followed by level three where we seek love and feelings of belonging. When we have achieved some satisfaction in those areas we move to create competence, prestige, and esteem in level four. Maslow says that when needs of existence, safety, love, and esteem have been met that we naturally tend toward what he calls self-actualization: the desire to become what we were designed to be, to rise to a level of creativity and of mental health that seeks peace, self-fulfillment, and oneness with God.

WISDOMONICS

I see people reach this level of understanding, but seldom by "self." I see people reach the level of MORE THAN ENOUGH, but never with "self" as the motivator. When the MORE THAN ENOUGH package comes together to cause a person to reach a level of maturity where he has become what God designed him to be, I call it *wisdomonics*. *Wisdomonics* is the gathering and processing of MORE THAN ENOUGH into a person, making them maximize, optimize, and reach through the top. It is the study of wealth and relationship building through the process of character development. *Wisdomonics* is real wisdom with movement. *Wisdomonics* is someone who has what the ancients called wisdom, which involves more than mere intellect. You are not self-actualized because you were not created by or for self; you are God-actualized and value-actualized, which empowers you beyond anything you could ever give yourself. *Wisdomonics* allows you to make correct decisions and gives you insight and the impetus for movement that is beyond your ability to dream up on your own. Proverbs 3:13 says, "Blessed is the man who finds wisdom, the man who gains understanding." Wisdom is not inside you waiting to come out; it is found by climbing the ladder to MORE THAN ENOUGH, learning and bringing into your life the process of

MORE THAN ENOUGH, and reaching out and becoming what you were created to be.

When you are walking in *wisdomonics* you have a feeling of abundance that gives you peace and makes you outwardly directed instead of being the selfish child we all start out as. Sometimes we touch *wisdomonics* for just a moment as we travel through life and then as we go further down the road to MORE THAN ENOUGH and are able to spend days in *wisdomonics*. Later as we are becoming more and more what we are supposed to be, we live entire months or years in *wisdomonics*.

CHECK THE TREE FOR FRUIT

When you are in *wisdomonics* you have several fruits to show for your journey. The MORE THAN ENOUGH package that we have built to this point is all present in your character if you are in *wisdomonics*. Your values are firm and are not a struggle for you. You don't have to think about whether something is right or wrong because you have visited your values map so many times it has become part of your being. Your vision and goals are clear and you know where you are going and why. The vision you are walking in lines up with, and flows clearly from, your values. You have unity in your relationships with mates, children, and team members. You will fight to protect that unity and oneness with those you love, and anyone or anything coming against that will be "in for a battle."

In *wisdomonics* you are always overflowing with hope. Your hope is so large and grows so quickly that it splashes on all those who come near you. Not some sappy candy apple hope, but the real kind that flows from values and vision. The kind of hope that is around *wisdomonics* is the kind that brings unspeakable joy. It is the kind of hope that survives critical blows, looks out through the years to come, and is inspired to walk through the hard day, the hard week, the hard month, or the hard year. *Wisdomonics* does not come, and will not stay, without the humility that leads you to be accountable to others who have also reached some type of *wisdomonics*. It is the humility that comes from knowing we all need support and encouragement so we are willing to accept that with grace, knowing that only a fool stands alone. When we stand alone we end our lives not in *wisdomonics,* but in bitterness and loneliness, wondering why we took the paths we took.

Wisdomonics always has an intensity to it that will push through the walls of the average and the normal because it does not come to the average or the normal. This is not an intensity of mere activity, or of anger, but an intensity that moves you whether others are moving or not. This kind of intensity is a hot blowtorch with a very large tank and a truck on the way to fill it again, a kind of intensity born of values, vision, and resting in *wisdomonics* that will not be denied. *Wisdomonics* can't come to you until you have a level of diligence, and diligence will always be magnified by your reaching *wisdomonics*. Wise people will always be patient; they aren't procrastinators, but they have a patience that allows them not to be forced into stupid actions. It is patience that sees the vision born of the values and that has as its sister intensity.

Contentment is a rung on the ladder that leads to *wisdomonics*. You can't experience and walk in true wisdom if you aren't content. When you meet someone who has reached *wisdomonics* you will always find someone with a deep sense of peace and contentment. This is not apathy; this is a peace with yourself, your surroundings, and God. Giving is something that you will always find where there is the depth of *wisdomonics*. Wise people are always giving people: They give of their stuff, they give of their time, and they give of themselves.

YOU GOTTA BE BRAVE

Someone who dives in front of a drunk driver risking his or her life to save a child is looked at with curiosity instead of admiration these days. The gerbils all stop their little wheels and look out with their heads cocked with curiosity, not understanding the courageous act because it is so far from where they live. Courage seems to be something that is not talked about much anymore. And yet courage is another key that always appears when you achieve *wisdomonics:* courage that causes you to stand up and be counted or causes you to move mountains. Courage born of wisdom is powerful courage, not just simply bravery, but deeply held real courage. It is courage that reflects values and stands firmly on them. Mahatma Gandhi said, "Cowards can never be moral."

Courage always gets you dirty; you have to be in the middle of the action to create action. In our intellectually sterile society, many times we would prefer to analyze as a spectator rather than take part as a doer. It is much easier to be on *Crossfire* than to be the subject of that night's program. As Theodore Roosevelt put it so eloquently:

> The credit belongs to the man who is actually in the arena; whose face is marred by dust, and sweat, and blood; who strives valiantly; who errs and comes short again and again; who knows the great enthusiasm, the great devotions, and spends himself in a worthy cause; who at the best knows in the end the triumph of high achievement; and who at worst, if he fails, at least he fails while daring greatly.

You can have all the other pieces of the puzzle and without courage you can't seem to find the energy to put the puzzle together. Courage is something we all should reach and strain for, and as we do, we realize that like all other character qualities we will find, there is pain in making them part of us. Sir Winston Churchill said, "Without courage, all other virtues lose their meaning." When you reach *wisdomonics* you will find that courage has become part of your makeup, not a boastful stupid arrogance, but a quiet courage that allows you to hold on when it seems no one else would or could.

HE WEARS HIS POWER SO LIGHTLY

One of my favorite lines comes from the movie *First Knight*. The film is a modern remake of *Camelot* complete with Sean Connery as the middle-aged King Arthur and Richard Gere as Sir Lancelot. Lady Guinevere is several years younger than King Arthur and is set to become his bride. When she is asked "Do you love him?" her response is what I see in people who have reached *wisdomonics*. She says, "How could I not love him, he wears his power so lightly, has such gentleness in his eyes." Quiet strength is to wear power lightly, understanding that power is just like money—it is only a tool to help others. The lion doesn't have to boast or wear pink hair like a strutting teenager to show he is the king of the jungle, he just is. The eagle doesn't have to prove his majesty, he just is. Quiet strength is needed today and is found only in folks who have made the whole package of *wisdomonics* part of their lives.

What happened to knowing that power is a privilege, not a weapon? I don't always handle the power given me well, but I always wish I could have quiet strength. Margaret Thatcher says, "Being powerful is like being a lady. If you have to tell people you are, you aren't." In a culture that seems to give respect to loud mouths, we seem to have labeled those with quiet strength as weak. The meek are considered weak, but this is an immature understanding of true meekness. Warren Weirsbe of Moody Bible College states this as well as I have ever heard, when he says, "Meekness is not weakness, it is power under control."

When we brought our second child home from the hospital our oldest, Denise, was a toddler, who thought her baby sister was a new doll. We let that little toddler hold the newborn only while sitting firmly on a chair with Mom or Dad nearby. We didn't let her carry her newborn sister all over the house or up and down stairs. Why? Well, you obviously know, she might have dropped poor Rachel. Denise loved her new sister and would not have done anything to hurt her on purpose, but she didn't have the strength to be gentle. You must have power to be truly gentle. I could easily carry my new daughter with love and compassion, but to physically care for her I had to have the strength to lift her gently. Real power is gentle, not boastful or rowdy like a wild teenager in a car with a big engine. Real power comes from *wisdomonics*, becoming what God designed you to be. The Bible says in Isaiah 30:15, "In quietness and in confidence shall be your strength."

BE DO HAVE

The spiritual boot camp, Momentous, teaches that we should function from the Be Do Have model of action. We should "Be" and let our "Do" flow from that which will lead us to "Have" what truly makes us whole. Too many times we try to shortcut and just "Do" to "Have" and we end up having the wrong things in our lives. If we will take the time to "Be" what is real, what is right, and what we were designed to "Be" before we "Do," we will naturally only "Do" what leads us toward what we should "Have." When you take the time to "Be" a MORE THAN ENOUGH person, you will always "Do" those things that flow from your vision and "Have" MORE THAN ENOUGH.

Wisdomonics comes when you have arrived at the true you, the you that you are destined to "Be." When you decide to "Be" before you act, you will act more decisively, accurately, and with more intensity because you are sure of your actions. Actions that are from *wisdomonics* are actions that come from confidence and courage, which were born way back there in values and vision. Stewart White says, "Do not attempt to do a thing unless you are sure of yourself; but do not relinquish it simply because someone else is not sure of you." Those folks who have achieved *wisdomonics* know criticism will come because they are folks who make things happen. When you are moving things around there are always small-minded, big-mouthed people who have something negative to say about you or your actions. I have never met anyone who did anything significant with his life that didn't get piles of criticism. Aristotle said, "Criticism is something we can avoid easily by doing nothing, saying nothing, and being nothing." Criticism makes someone who has reached *wisdomonics* take note and sometimes gets his feelings hurt, but he checks against his values and vision, patches up his hope, and then goes right back after something.

IT ALL COMES TOGETHER

Wisdomonics is the whole package and progression of the proven keys of MORE THAN ENOUGH. As you have walked through the process presented in this book you have been reaching for *wisdomonics*. The abundance that comes to your relationships can't help but show up in your finances. MORE THAN ENOUGH is about understanding that wealth building and relationships are so tightly wrapped around each other that to not build both at once virtually guarantees your failure, which leaves you at just average, just regular, and just another name on a tombstone. MORE THAN ENOUGH is about packaging the building blocks and the progression of these keys into your heart, your head, and your spirit. I can assure you that as you implement both the easy and the gut-wrenching changes that we all must go through to finally have some level and consistency of *wisdomonics*, you will have MORE THAN ENOUGH.

NOW WHAT?

I have just poured years of experience and the wisdom of scholars, theologians, and philosophers into your life. Now what are you going to do? Are you going to put this book on a shelf with all the other "good books" you have read, or are you going to take these proven building blocks and go about building a MORE THAN ENOUGH life that will be so full you feel like bursting? Reread the chapters, write all over this book, make these principals part of your life, reread the Keys to the MORE THAN ENOUGH Mansion sections every week for a year to make sure you are on your way to MORE THAN ENOUGH. These are not mere concepts, they are life-changing and life-giving building blocks, but only if you choose to build. Please don't be average, begin your travels down the road to MORE THAN ENOUGH, and I hope I'll see you at the top!

THE STORY ENDS, OR IS IT JUST BEGINNING?

Out of core *values, vision* is born. *Vision* is put into work clothes and becomes *goals.* Shared *goals* give you *unity* with those who are on the journey with you. *Values, vision,* and *unity* repair broken *hope* and build *hope* into the fuel that fires the rocket of *intensity.* The rocket of *intensity* is kept between the ditches by *accountability* and *support.* The pilot of the rocket ensuring that *intensity* stays on *vision's* course is *diligence.* His copilot and navigator are *work* and *discipline. Patience* that is born of power has at its center *intensity, hope, vision,* and *diligence.* You can't have real *patience* without first having those things and when you have it relationships are built and you add yet more *unity. Contentment* changes your *vision,* gives you a different kind of *intensity,* definitely fuels *patience, diligence,* and *unity* while it is also born of all those things. *Giving* is the result of *values* and the *vision* they bring. *Unity* is increased by *giving* because relationships are affected. You always have more *hope* when pouring your life into something that matters. Part of the great misunderstanding is that somehow *giving* is the act of someone who isn't *intense* or *diligent* when in fact the opposite is true. *Patience* and *contentment* rise to a whole new level of understanding when they bring on *giving,* which then in turn feeds you more of each of those. Slowly we have built with the proven building blocks to MORE THAN ENOUGH and as we reach the top we discover *wisdomonics,* the gathering and using of all the list and processes to live life to overflowing levels by becoming all God made you to be. Go for it!

Thoughts from Sharon . . .

Well, have you learned all that you can about **MORE THAN ENOUGH**? *If you read through this book in a hurry, go back and take your time and enjoy it again. There is so much valuable information to be learned.*

The lessons we learned were hard and sometimes I wish we had not learned them the way we did. Yet without these lessons we would never have received the blessing that enables us to be able to help others. Hopefully, it will do the same for you.

My prayer for you is that you have gained wisdom and hope from reading this book. Now take the next step. Be a giver, encourage someone else who needs help, and be what you know God had in mind for you when he created you. Hope, wisdom, understanding, humility, and many more attributes are at your disposal. Use them well.

Keys to the More Than Enough Mansion

1. Change is very hard and we change only when the pain of *same* is greater than the pain of change.
2. Cleansing cries and hinge pins are signals that we are ready.
3. Values really do matter and real values are the foundation of everything to come.
4. Integrity—real deep integrity, even with the little things—is vital because deception destroys.
5. Connectedness is key; take time to use the sidewalks that connect you to family, friends, and coworkers.
6. Vision that is rooted in values is the only vision that will last.
7. Vision makes you a long-term investor, not living for the moment.
8. Goals are the building blocks of vision, vision in work clothes.
9. Model for and teach your children about vision and goals.
10. Opposites attract and men and women are different; identify and admit those differences and use each other's strengths for MORE THAN ENOUGH.
11. Men, build an emergency fund and leave it alone; it will change the way your wife treats you.
12. Budgeting together brings tremendous oneness

to your marriage, but you must die to selfishness; the "you" in "unity" must be silent.

13. Hope is lost when it is placed in people, stuff, and institutions.

14. Hope is lost when we believe failure is permanent and we lose perspective.

15. Hope is an act of the will and moves people to action.

16. Return to strong values and the vision born of them to rekindle your hope.

17. Small groups for support and encouragement are the most powerful form of behavior modification known.

18. When holding your spouse accountable use "I feel" statements that aren't so threatening.

19. Pride busting and encouragement when needed are the lost art of the mentor.

20. To reach MORE THAN ENOUGH you have to be as intense as the gazelle is when running from the cheetah: gazelle intensity.

21. Gazelle intensity given focus will create momentum, and momentum in relationships and wealth building brings almost inexplicable illogical things into your life.

22. Work is doing it, discipline is doing it every day, and diligence is doing it well every day.

23. No one has MORE THAN ENOUGH in relationships or

wealth without hard work, discipline, and diligence.

24. Patience is golden and like gold is purified in the fires of life.

25. Patience brings real power to your wealth building and a real quality to your relationships because you are looking long term.

26. Patience makes you an investor who stays in the market and reaps long-term rewards, and patience demands you save to pay cash so you can avoid debt.

27. Contentment is possibly the most powerful financial principle; with it, getting out of debt, saving, and giving are easy.

28. Watch for the thieves of contentment: the extreme level of marketing in our culture that makes us want more, envy, and get-rich-quick and appear-rich-quick schemes.

29. You won't be happy when. . . . Happiness is a decision to be content where you are now; don't confuse fun and happiness.

30. The great misunderstanding is that we think we have to hoard to get, when in reality you can only have MORE THAN ENOUGH by releasing ownership spiritually and emotionally, then showing that by giving time and money away.

31. The most pure joy you will ever experience is to

give your time and your money because you were designed to be a giver by God, you were made in His image.

32. As we reach the top, we discover *wisdomonics,* the gathering and using of all the traits and processes that will allow you to live life to over-flowing levels by becoming all that God made you to be. Go for it!

APPENDIX

Financial Forms

Work Sheet 1

Major Components of a
Healthy Financial Plan

	ACTION NEEDED	ACTION DATE
Written Cash Flow Plan		
Will and/or Estate Elan		
Debt Reduction Plan		
Tax Reduction Plan		
Emergency Funding		
Retirement Funding		
College Funding		
Charitable Giving		
Teach My Children		
Life Insurance		
Health Insurance		
Disability Insurance		
Auto Insurance		
Homeowner's Insurance		

I, _____ , a responsible adult, do hereby
swear to take the above-stated actions by the above-stated dates to financially secure the well-being of my family and myself. (copy to spouse)

Signed: _____   Date: _____

Work Sheet 2

Consumer Equity Work Sheet

ITEM / DESCRIBE	VALUE	−	DEBT	=	EQUITY
Real Estate _____	_____		_____		_____
Real Estate _____	_____		_____		_____
Car _____	_____		_____		_____
Car _____	_____		_____		_____
Cash on Hand	_____		_____		_____
Checking Account	_____		_____		_____
Checking Account	_____		_____		_____
Savings Account	_____		_____		_____
Savings Account	_____		_____		_____
Money Market Account	_____		_____		_____
Mutual Funds	_____		_____		_____
Retirement Plan	_____		_____		_____
Stocks or Bonds	_____		_____		_____
Cash Value (Insurance)	_____		_____		_____
Household Items	_____		_____		_____
Jewelry	_____		_____		_____
Antiques	_____		_____		_____
Boat	_____		_____		_____
Unsecured Debt (Negative)	_____		_____		_____
Credit Card Debt (Negative)	_____		_____		_____
Other _____	_____		_____		_____
Other _____	_____		_____		_____
Other _____	_____		_____		_____
TOTAL	_____		_____		_____

Work Sheet 3

Income Sources

SOURCE	AMOUNT	PERIOD / DESCRIBE
Salary 1		
Salary 2		
Salary 3		
Bonus		
Self-Employment		
Interest Income		
Dividend Income		
Royalty Income		
Rents		
Notes		
Alimony		
Child Support		
AFDC		
Unemployment		
Social Security		
Pension		
Annuity		
Disability Income		
Cash Gifts		
Trust Fund		
Other ————		
Other ————		
Other ————		
Other ————		
TOTAL		

Work Sheet 4

Lump Sum Payment Planning

Payments you make on a nonmonthly basis can be budget busters, if you do not plan for them. Here you will convert these to a monthly basis for use on Work Sheet 5. Then you will set money aside monthly to avoid strain or borrowing when these events occur. If an item here is already paid monthly, enter NA. If you make a payment quarterly, then annualize it for this work sheet.

ITEM NEEDED	ANNUAL AMOUNT		MONTHLY AMOUNT
Real Estate Taxes	_____	÷ 12 =	_____
Homeowner's Ins.	_____	÷ 12 =	_____
Home Repairs	_____	÷ 12 =	_____
Replace Furniture	_____	÷ 12 =	_____
Medical Bills	_____	÷ 12 =	_____
Health Insurance	_____	÷ 12 =	_____
Life Insurance	_____	÷ 12 =	_____
Disability Insurance	_____	÷ 12 =	_____
Car Insurance	_____	÷ 12 =	_____
Car Repair/Tags	_____	÷ 12 =	_____
Replace Car	_____	÷ 12 =	_____
Clothing	_____	÷ 12 =	_____
Tuition	_____	÷ 12 =	_____
Bank Note	_____	÷ 12 =	_____
IRS (Self-Employed)	_____	÷ 12 =	_____
Vacation	_____	÷ 12 =	_____
Gifts (inc. Christmas)	_____	÷ 12 =	_____
Other _____	_____	÷ 12 =	_____
Other _____	_____	÷ 12 =	_____

Monthly Cash Flow Plan

Every dollar of your income should be allocated to some category on this monthly cash flow plan. Money "left over" should be put back into a category even if you make up a new category. You should make spending decisions ahead of time. Almost every category (except debt) should have some dollar amount in it. For example, if you do not plan to replace the furniture, when you need to do so in the future your finances will be strained and you will need to borrow. Plan for that expense now by saving for it. I have actually had people tell me that they can do without clothing. (Oh, come on!) Be careful too in your zeal to make the numbers work that you don't substitute the urgent for the important.

Fill in the amount for each subcategory under "Subtotal" and then the total for each main category under "Total." As you go through your first month, fill in the "Actually Spent" column with your real expenses or the savings you had for that area. If there is a substantial difference in the plan versus the reality, something has to change. You will either have to adjust the amount allocated to that area up and another down, or you will have to better control your spending in that area.

In the column "% of Take-Home Pay," write in the percentage of your total take-home pay that you spent on a particular category, such as "Housing." Then you can compare your percentages with those on Work Sheet 6 to determine if you need to consider adjusting your lifestyle.

IMPORTANT (1): Emergency fund should get all the savings until three to six months of expenses have been saved.

NOTE: Savings should be increased as you get closer to being debt free.

HINT: By saving early for Christmas and other gifts, you can get great buys and give better gifts for the same money.

BUDGETED

ITEM	SUB-TOTAL	TOTAL	ACTUALLY SPENT	% of TAKE-HOME PAY
CHARITABLE GIFTS		_____	_____	_____
SAVING				
Emergency Fund (1)	_____		_____	
Retirement Fund	_____		_____	
College Fund	_____	_____	_____	_____
HOUSING				
First Mortgage	_____		_____	
Second Mortgage	_____		_____	
Real Estate Taxes	_____		_____	
Homeowner's Ins.	_____		_____	
Repairs or Mnt. Fee	_____		_____	
Replace Furniture	_____		_____	
Other	_____	_____	_____	_____
UTILITIES				
Electricity	_____		_____	
Water	_____		_____	
Gas	_____		_____	
Phone	_____		_____	
Trash	_____		_____	
Cable	_____	_____	_____	_____
FOOD				
Grocery	_____		_____	
Restaurants	_____	_____	_____	_____

PAGE 1 TOTAL   _____ _____

Work Sheet 5 *(continued)*

BUDGETED

ITEM	SUB-TOTAL	TOTAL	ACTUALLY SPENT	% of TAKE-HOME PAY
TRANSPORTATION				
Car Payment	_____		_____	
Car Payment	_____		_____	
Gas and Oil	_____		_____	
Repairs and Tires	_____		_____	
Car Insurance	_____		_____	
License and Taxes	_____		_____	
Car Replacement	_____	_____	_____	_____
CLOTHING				
Children	_____		_____	
Adults	_____		_____	
Cleaning/Laundry	_____	_____	_____	_____
MEDICAL/HEALTH				
Disability Ins.	_____		_____	
Health Insurance	_____		_____	
Doctor Bills	_____		_____	
Dentist	_____		_____	
Optometrist	_____		_____	
Drugs	_____	_____	_____	_____
PERSONAL				
Life Insurance	_____		_____	
Child Care	_____		_____	
PAGE 2 TOTAL		_____	_____	

Work Sheet 5 *(continued)*

BUDGETED

ITEM	SUB-TOTAL	TOTAL	ACTUALLY SPENT	% of TAKE-HOME PAY
PERSONAL *(continued)*				
Baby-sitter	_____		_____	
Toiletries	_____		_____	
Cosmetics	_____		_____	
Hair Care	_____		_____	
Education/Adult	_____		_____	
School Tuition	_____		_____	
School Supplies	_____		_____	
Child Support	_____		_____	
Alimony	_____		_____	
Subscriptions	_____		_____	
Organization Dues	_____		_____	
Gifts (inc. Christmas)	_____		_____	
Miscellaneous	_____		_____	
Blow $$	_____	_____	_____	_____
RECREATION				
Entertainment	_____		_____	
Vacation	_____	_____	_____	_____
DEBTS (Hopefully $0)				
Visa 1	_____		_____	
Visa 2	_____		_____	
MasterCard 1	_____		_____	
MasterCard 2	_____		_____	
PAGE 3 TOTAL		_____	_____	

Work Sheet 5 *(continued)*

BUDGETED

ITEM	SUB-TOTAL	TOTAL	ACTUALLY SPENT	% of TAKE-HOME PAY
DEBTS (Hopefully $0) *(continued)*				
American Express	_____		_____	
DiscoverCard	_____		_____	
Gas Card 1	_____		_____	
Gas Card 2	_____		_____	
Dept. Store Card 1	_____		_____	
Dept. Store Card 2	_____		_____	
Finance Co. 1	_____		_____	
Finance Co. 2	_____		_____	
Credit Line	_____		_____	
Student Loan 1	_____		_____	
Student Loan 2	_____		_____	
Other _____	_____		_____	
Other _____	_____		_____	
Other _____	_____		_____	
Other _____	_____		_____	
Other _____	_____	_____	_____	_____
PAGE 4 TOTAL		_____	_____	
PAGE 3 TOTAL		_____	_____	
PAGE 2 TOTAL		_____	_____	
PAGE 1 TOTAL		_____	_____	
GRAND TOTAL		_____	_____	
TOTAL INCOME	minus	_____	_____	
DIFFERENCE		Zero	_____	

Work Sheet 6

Recommended Percentages

I have used a compilation of several sources and my own experience to derive the suggested percentage guidelines. However, these are only recommended percentages and will change dramatically if you have a very high or very low income. For instance, if you have a very low income, your necessities percentages will be high. If you have a high income, your necessities will be a lower percentage of income and hopefully savings (not debt) will be higher than recommended.

ITEM	ACTUAL %	RECOMMENDED %
Charitable Gifts	_____	10–15%
Saving	_____	5–10%
Housing	_____	25–35%
Utilities	_____	5–10%
Food	_____	5–15%
Transportation	_____	10–15%
Clothing	_____	2–7%
Medical/Health	_____	5–10%
Personal	_____	5–10%
Recreation	_____	5–10%
Debts	_____	5–10%

Sample Allocated Spending Plan

Work Sheet 7

Sample Allocated Spending Plan

This work sheet is where all your work thus far starts giving you some peace. You will implement your Work Sheet 5 information into your life, going from theory to reality, by using Work Sheet 7. (Please note: If you have an irregular income, like self-employment or commissions, you should use Work Sheet 8, after reviewing Work Sheet 7.)

There are four columns to distribute as many as four different incomes within one month. Each column is one pay period. If you are a one-income household and you get paid two times per month, then you will use only two columns. If both spouses work and one is paid weekly and the other every two weeks, add the two paychecks together on the weeks you both get a paycheck and list the one paycheck on the other two. Date the pay period columns and then enter the income for that period. As you allocate your paycheck to an item, put the remaining balance to the right of the slash. Some bills will come out of each pay period and some only on selected pay periods. As an example, you may take "Car Gas" out of every paycheck, but you may pay the electric bill from period 2. You already pay some bills or make payments out of designated checks; now you pay all things from designated checks.

The whole point to this work sheet, which is the culmination of all your monthly planning, is to allocate or "spend" your whole paycheck before you get paid. I don't care where you allocate your money, but you must allocate all of it before you get your check. Now all the tense, crisislike symptoms have been removed because you planned. No more management by crisis or impulse. Those who tend to be impulsive should just allocate more to the "Blow" category. At least you are now doing it on purpose and not by default. The last blank that you make an entry in should have a 0 to the right of the slash, showing you have allocated your whole check.

Work Sheet 7

PAY PERIOD   _____ _____ _____ _____

ITEM

INCOME   _____ _____ _____ _____

CHARITABLE   ___/___ ___/___ ___/___ ___/___

SAVING

   Emergency Fund   ___/___ ___/___ ___/___ ___/___

   Retirement Fund   ___/___ ___/___ ___/___ ___/___

   College Fund   ___/___ ___/___ ___/___ ___/___

HOUSING

   First Mortgage   ___/___ ___/___ ___/___ ___/___

   Second Mortgage   ___/___ ___/___ ___/___ ___/___

   Real Estate Taxes   ___/___ ___/___ ___/___ ___/___

   Homeowner's Ins.   ___/___ ___/___ ___/___ ___/___

   Repairs/Mnt. Fees   ___/___ ___/___ ___/___ ___/___

   Replace Furniture   ___/___ ___/___ ___/___ ___/___

   Other _____   ___/___ ___/___ ___/___ ___/___

UTILITIES

   Electricity   ___/___ ___/___ ___/___ ___/___

   Water   ___/___ ___/___ ___/___ ___/___

   Gas   ___/___ ___/___ ___/___ ___/___

   Phone   ___/___ ___/___ ___/___ ___/___

Work Sheet 7 *(continued)*

UTILITIES *(continued)*

   Trash   ___/___   ___/___   ___/___   ___/___

   Cable   ___/___   ___/___   ___/___   ___/___

FOOD

   Grocery   ___/___   ___/___   ___/___   ___/___

   Restaurants   ___/___   ___/___   ___/___   ___/___

TRANSPORTATION

   Car Payment   ___/___   ___/___   ___/___   ___/___

   Car Payment   ___/___   ___/___   ___/___   ___/___

   Gas & Oil   ___/___   ___/___   ___/___   ___/___

   Repairs & Tires   ___/___   ___/___   ___/___   ___/___

   Car Insurance   ___/___   ___/___   ___/___   ___/___

   License & Taxes   ___/___   ___/___   ___/___   ___/___

   Car Replacement   ___/___   ___/___   ___/___   ___/___

CLOTHING

   Children   ___/___   ___/___   ___/___   ___/___

   Adults   ___/___   ___/___   ___/___   ___/___

   Cleaning/Lndry.   ___/___   ___/___   ___/___   ___/___

MEDICAL/HEALTH

   Disability Ins.   ___/___   ___/___   ___/___   ___/___

   Health Insurance   ___/___   ___/___   ___/___   ___/___

   Doctor   ___/___   ___/___   ___/___   ___/___

   Dentist   ___/___   ___/___   ___/___   ___/___

   Optometrist   ___/___   ___/___   ___/___   ___/___

   Drugs   ___/___   ___/___   ___/___   ___/___

Work Sheet 7 *(continued)*

PERSONAL

Life Insurance ____/____ ____/____ ____/____ ____/____

Child Care ____/____ ____/____ ____/____ ____/____

Baby-sitter ____/____ ____/____ ____/____ ____/____

Toiletries ____/____ ____/____ ____/____ ____/____

Cosmetics ____/____ ____/____ ____/____ ____/____

Hair Care ____/____ ____/____ ____/____ ____/____

Education/Adult ____/____ ____/____ ____/____ ____/____

School Tuition ____/____ ____/____ ____/____ ____/____

School Supplies ____/____ ____/____ ____/____ ____/____

Child Support ____/____ ____/____ ____/____ ____/____

Alimony ____/____ ____/____ ____/____ ____/____

Subscriptions ____/____ ____/____ ____/____ ____/____

Organization Dues ____/____ ____/____ ____/____ ____/____

Gifts (inc. Christmas) ____/____ ____/____ ____/____ ____/____

Miscellaneous ____/____ ____/____ ____/____ ____/____

Blow $$ ____/____ ____/____ ____/____ ____/____

RECREATION

Entertainment ____/____ ____/____ ____/____ ____/____

Vacation ____/____ ____/____ ____/____ ____/____

DEBTS (Hopefully $0)

Visa 1 ____/____ ____/____ ____/____ ____/____

Visa 2 ____/____ ____/____ ____/____ ____/____

MasterCard 1 ____/____ ____/____ ____/____ ____/____

MasterCard 2 ____/____ ____/____ ____/____ ____/____

Work Sheet 7 *(continued)*

DEBTS (Hopefully $0) *(continued)*

Amer. Express	___/___	___/___	___/___	___/___
DiscoverCard	___/___	___/___	___/___	___/___
Gas Card 1	___/___	___/___	___/___	___/___
Gas Card 2	___/___	___/___	___/___	___/___
Dept. Store Card 1	___/___	___/___	___/___	___/___
Dept. Store Card 2	___/___	___/___	___/___	___/___
Finance Co. 1	___/___	___/___	___/___	___/___
Finance Co. 2	___/___	___/___	___/___	___/___
Credit Line	___/___	___/___	___/___	___/___
Student Loan 1	___/___	___/___	___/___	___/___
Student Loan 2	___/___	___/___	___/___	___/___
Other _____	___/___	___/___	___/___	___/___
Other _____	___/___	___/___	___/___	___/___
Other _____	___/___	___/___	___/___	___/___
Other _____	___/___	___/___	___/___	___/___
Other _____	___/___	___/___	___/___	___/___

Irregular Income Planning

Many of us have irregular incomes. If you are self-employed, as I am, or work on commission or royalties, then planning your expenses is difficult, since you cannot always predict your income. You should, however, still do all the work sheets except Work Sheet 7. Work Sheet 5 will tell you what you have to earn monthly to survive or prosper, and those real numbers are very good for goal setting.

What you must do is to take the items on Work Sheet 5 and prioritize them by importance. Remember, by importance, not urgency. You should ask yourself, "If I have only enough money to pay one thing, what would that be?" Then ask, "If I have only enough money to pay one more thing, what will that be?" And so on down the list. Now, be prepared to stand your ground because things have a way of seeming important when they are not. Saving should be a high priority.

The third column, "Cumulative Amount," is the total of all amounts above that item. So if you get a $2,000 check, you can see how far down your priority list you can go.

ITEM	AMOUNT	CUMULATIVE AMOUNT
_____	_____	_____
_____	_____	_____
_____	_____	_____
_____	_____	_____
_____	_____	_____
_____	_____	_____
_____	_____	_____
_____	_____	_____

Work Sheet 8 *(continued)*

ITEM	AMOUNT	CUMULATIVE AMOUNT

Work Sheet 9

Breakdown of Savings

As you save for certain items such as furniture, car replacement, home maintenance, or clothes, your savings balance will grow. This sheet is designed to remind you that all of that money is committed to something, not just a Hawaiian vacation on impulse because you are now "rich." Keep up with your breakdown of savings monthly for one quarter at a time.

ITEM	BALANCE BY MONTH:		
Emergency Fund (1)			
Retirement Fund			
College Fund			
Real Estate Taxes			
Homeowner's Insurance			
Repairs or Mnt. Fee			
Replace Furniture			
Car Insurance			
Car Replacement			
Disability Insurance			
Health Insurance			
Doctor			
Dentist			
Optometrist			
Life Insurance			
School Tuition			
School Supplies			
Gifts (inc. Christmas)			
Vacation			
Other _____			
Other _____			
Other _____			
TOTAL			

Work Sheet 10

The Debt Snowball

List your debts in descending order with the smallest payoff or balance first. Do not be concerned with interest rates or terms unless two debts have similar payoffs; then list the higher interest-rate debt first. Paying the little debts off first shows you quick feedback, and you are more likely to stay with the plan.

Redo this work sheet each time you pay off a debt so you can see how close you are getting to freedom. Keep the old work sheets to wallpaper the bathroom in your new debt-free house. The "New Payment" is found by adding all the payments on the debts listed above that item to the payment you are working on, so you have compounding payments, which will get you out of debt very quickly. "Payments Remaining" is the number of payments remaining when you get down the snowball to that item. "Cumulative Payments" is the total payments needed, including the snowball, to pay off that item. In other words, this is your running total for "Payments Remaining."

Date: _____ Countdown to freedom

ITEM	TOTAL PAYOFF	MINIMUM PYMT.	NEW PYMT.	PYMTS. REMAINING	CUMULATIVE PYMTS.
_____	_____	_____	_____	_____	_____
_____	_____	_____	_____	_____	_____
_____	_____	_____	_____	_____	_____
_____	_____	_____	_____	_____	_____
_____	_____	_____	_____	_____	_____
_____	_____	_____	_____	_____	_____
_____	_____	_____	_____	_____	_____
_____	_____	_____	_____	_____	_____
_____	_____	_____	_____	_____	_____

Work Sheet 10 *(continued)*

ITEM	TOTAL PAYOFF	MINIMUM PYMT.	NEW PYMT.	PYMTS. REMAINING	CUMULATIVE PYMTS.

Retirement Monthly Planning

In order to retire with some security, you must aim at something. Too many people use the *ready, fire, aim* approach to retirement planning. Your assignment is to determine how much per month you should be saving at 12 percent interest in order to retire at sixty-five years old with what you need.

If you are saving at 12 percent and inflation is at 4 percent, then you are moving ahead of inflation at a net of 8 percent per year. If you invest your nest egg at retirement at 12 percent and want to break even with 4 percent inflation, you will be living on 8 percent income.

STEP ONE:

Annual income (today) you wish to retire on $ _____

divided by   _____.08_____

(nest egg needed)   equals $ _____

STEP TWO:

To achieve that nest egg, you will save at 12 percent, netting 8 percent after inflation, so we will target that nest egg using 8 percent.

_____ × _____ = _____

   Nest Egg Needed   Factor Monthly   Savings Needed

8% factors (select the one that matches your age)

Age	Years to Save	Factor
25	40	.000286
30	35	.000436
35	30	.000671
40	25	.001051
45	20	.001698
50	15	.002890
55	10	.005466
60	5	.013610

NOTE: If you have any doubts about saving now, take a look at what happens if you delay saving for five or ten years.

Pro Rata Plan

If you cannot pay your creditors what they request, you should treat them all fairly and the same. You should pay even the ones who are jerks, and pay everyone as much as you can. Many creditors will accept a written plan and cut special deals with you as long as you are communicating, maybe even overcommunicating, and sending them something. We have had clients using this plan who have sent only $2 and have survived literally for years.

Pro rata means their share—the percentage of your total debt they are owed determines how much you send them. You send the check with a budget and this work sheet attached each month even if the creditor says they will not accept it.

ITEM	TOTAL PAYOFF	÷ TOTAL DEBT	= PERCENT	DISPOSABLE × INCOME	NEW = PAYMENTS
_____	_____ ÷ _____		=. _____	× _____	= _____
_____	_____ ÷ _____		=. _____	× _____	= _____
_____	_____ ÷ _____		=. _____	× _____	= _____
_____	_____ ÷ _____		=. _____	× _____	= _____
_____	_____ ÷ _____		=. _____	× _____	= _____
_____	_____ ÷ _____		=. _____	× _____	= _____
_____	_____ ÷ _____		=. _____	× _____	= _____
_____	_____ ÷ _____		=. _____	× _____	= _____
_____	_____ ÷ _____		=. _____	× _____	= _____
_____	_____ ÷ _____		=. _____	× _____	= _____
_____	_____ ÷ _____		=. _____	× _____	= _____
_____	_____ ÷ _____		=. _____	× _____	= _____
_____	_____ ÷ _____		=. _____	× _____	= _____
_____	_____ ÷ _____		=. _____	× _____	= _____
_____	_____ ÷ _____		=. _____	× _____	= _____
_____	_____ ÷ _____		=. _____	× _____	= _____

Work Sheet 12 *(continued)*

ITEM	TOTAL PAYOFF	÷ TOTAL DEBT	= PERCENT	DISPOSABLE × INCOME	NEW = PAYMENTS
_____	_____ ÷ _____		=._____	×_____	=_____
_____	_____ ÷ _____		=._____	×_____	=_____
_____	_____ ÷ _____		=._____	×_____	=_____
_____	_____ ÷ _____		=._____	×_____	=_____
_____	_____ ÷ _____		=._____	×_____	=_____
_____	_____ ÷ _____		=._____	×_____	=_____
_____	_____ ÷ _____		=._____	×_____	=_____
_____	_____ ÷ _____		=._____	×_____	=_____
_____	_____ ÷ _____		=._____	×_____	=_____
_____	_____ ÷ _____		=._____	×_____	=_____
_____	_____ ÷ _____		=._____	×_____	=_____
_____	_____ ÷ _____		=._____	×_____	=_____
_____	_____ ÷ _____		=._____	×_____	=_____
_____	_____ ÷ _____		=._____	×_____	=_____
_____	_____ ÷ _____		=._____	×_____	=_____
_____	_____ ÷ _____		=._____	×_____	=_____
_____	_____ ÷ _____		=._____	×_____	=_____
_____	_____ ÷ _____		=._____	×_____	=_____
_____	_____ ÷ _____		=._____	×_____	=_____
_____	_____ ÷ _____		=._____	×_____	=_____
_____	_____ ÷ _____		=._____	×_____	=_____
_____	_____ ÷ _____		=._____	×_____	=_____
_____	_____ ÷ _____		=._____	×_____	=_____
_____	_____ ÷ _____		=._____	×_____	=_____
_____	_____ ÷ _____		=._____	×_____	=_____
_____	_____ ÷ _____		=._____	×_____	=_____
_____	_____ ÷ _____		=._____	×_____	=_____

Work Sheet 12 *(continued)*

ITEM	TOTAL PAYOFF	TOTAL ÷ DEBT	= PERCENT	DISPOSABLE × INCOME	NEW = PAYMENTS
_____	_____ ÷	_____	=. _____	× _____	= _____
_____	_____ ÷	_____	=. _____	× _____	= _____
_____	_____ ÷	_____	=. _____	× _____	= _____
_____	_____ ÷	_____	=. _____	× _____	= _____
_____	_____ ÷	_____	=. _____	× _____	= _____
_____	_____ ÷	_____	=. _____	× _____	= _____
_____	_____ ÷	_____	=. _____	× _____	= _____
_____	_____ ÷	_____	=. _____	× _____	= _____
_____	_____ ÷	_____	=. _____	× _____	= _____
_____	_____ ÷	_____	=. _____	× _____	= _____
_____	_____ ÷	_____	=. _____	× _____	= _____
_____	_____ ÷	_____	=. _____	× _____	= _____
_____	_____ ÷	_____	=. _____	× _____	= _____
_____	_____ ÷	_____	=. _____	× _____	= _____
_____	_____ ÷	_____	=. _____	× _____	= _____
_____	_____ ÷	_____	=. _____	× _____	= _____
_____	_____ ÷	_____	=. _____	× _____	= _____
_____	_____ ÷	_____	=. _____	× _____	= _____
_____	_____ ÷	_____	=. _____	× _____	= _____
_____	_____ ÷	_____	=. _____	× _____	= _____
_____	_____ ÷	_____	=. _____	× _____	= _____
_____	_____ ÷	_____	=. _____	× _____	= _____
_____	_____ ÷	_____	=. _____	× _____	= _____
_____	_____ ÷	_____	=. _____	× _____	= _____
_____	_____ ÷	_____	=. _____	× _____	= _____

SELECTED BIBLIOGRAPHY

Alderman, Lesley. "When You Sacrifice Your Future for Your Kids," *Money,* March 1998, pp. 69–74.

Carter, Jaine, and James D. Carter, "Relationships: Communication Can Pay Off in Fewer Fights About Money," *Holland News Service.* www.detnews.com, July 15, 1997.

Chilton, David. *The Wealthy Barber: Everyone's Commonsense Guide to Becoming Financially Independent,* 3rd edition. USA: Prima Publishers, 1998.

Dart, Bob, "All's Not Well with American Family; Poverty and Divorce Rampant," *The American Journal and Constitution,* January 17, 1991, G10.

Gray, John, Ph.D. *Men Are from Mars, Women Are from Venus.* New York: HarperCollins, 1992.

Gwynne, Robert, "Maslow's Hierarchy of Needs," funnelweb.utcc.utk.edu.

Hall, Cindy, and Tammi Wark, "Then vs. Now: How Families Fare," *USA Today,* June 19, 1996, 2B.

Hybels, Bill, and Rob Wilkins. *Descending into Greatness.* Grand Rapids, MI: Zondervan Publishing House, 1993.

Kallestad, Walt. *The Everyday Anytime Guide to Christian Leadership.* Minneapolis, MN: Augsburg, 1995.

Mays, Carl. *A Strategy for Winning.* New York: The Lincoln Bradley Publishing Group, 1991.

"Money Talks. We Listened," *Worth,* June 1994, p. 69.

Ronsvalle, John L., and Sylcia Ronsvalle. *The State of Church Giving Through 1995.* Champaign, IL: Empty Tomb, Inc., 1997.

Schor, Julian, "Julian Schor on the Overspent American," transcript from May 20, 1999, www.time.com.

Smalley, Gary. *Making Love Last Forever.* U.S.: Gary Smalley, 1996.

Stanley, Thomas J., and William D. Danko. *The Millionaire Next Door.* Marietta, GA: Longstreet Press, Inc., 1996.

"Statistics about 'Deadbeat Dads' and the Effects of Absent Fathers," http://www.vix/pub/men/nofather/dart.html.

Sutton, Remar. *Don't Get Taken Every Time.* New York: Penguin Books, 1983.

TV Free America, "Statistics on Television's Impact," August 20, 1998, www.tvfa.org.

"Why Money Is the Leading Cause of Divorce," *Jet,* November 18, 1996, pp. 34–37.

If you would like to hear *The Dave Ramsey Show* in your area, please send the following form letter to the program director at your local talk-radio station:

(Today's date)

(Your Name)
(Your Street Address)
(Your City, State, Zip)

Attn: Program Director
(Your Talk-Radio Station's Call Letters)
(Street Address)
(City, State, Zip)

Dear Program Director:

I am writing you to ask you to listen to an informative and entertaining program, *The Dave Ramsey Show*. This call-in talk show is about life, love, and the pursuit of piles of cash. This show discusses personal finances as they revolve around life, marriage, work, and retirement.

It is entirely different from the typical financial show; it's entertaining, not stuffy. The host doesn't talk down to the callers for the mistakes they've made, but rather offers them steps to correct their mistakes and hope for a better future.

You can listen to the show on their call-in line at 888-GAME TIP, Monday through Friday, 1–4 P.M., CST. For syndication information call 888-22PEACE ext. 114. Please give them a call and listen to the show and please add *The Dave Ramsey Show* to your line-up immediately.

Thank you for your attention to this matter and for considering *The Dave Ramsey Show*.

Sincerely,

(Your Name)

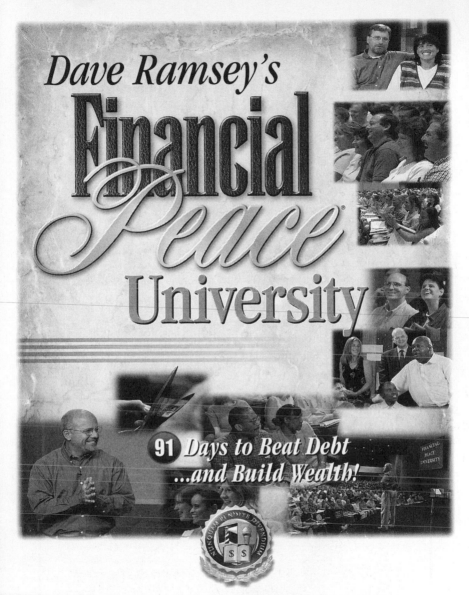

Dave Ramsey's
Financial Peace University

91 Days to Beat Debt ...and Build Wealth!

Learn how to bring this Life-Changing Program to
your community... or to get started in a class today, call

1-888-22-PEACE

Check us out on the web at:
www.daveramsey.com

The Lampo Group Educational Material

We offer a 90-day satisfaction guarantee on all our products.

Financial Peace "Cash Flow Planning"

This 60-minute cassette enables viewers to gain complete understanding of the components involved in setting up their cash flow plan. This session requires the use of the *Financial Peace* book.

VHS Videocassette: $19.95   **Audiocassette: $9.95**

Financial Peace "Dumping Debt"

This 60-minute cassette provides techniques on "dumping debt." Not just a portion of your debt . . . but ALL OF IT!—by teaching the viewer a unique way of "snowballing" those debts.

VHS Videocassette: $19.95   **Audiocassette: $9.95**

The FPU Envelope System

Easy-to-carry pocket-size binder with clasp, including 10 envelopes, extra recording sheets, and instructions to implement the envelope system outlined in the book *Financial Peace*.

$15.00

To see all of our great products go to **www.daveramsey.com**

Make checks payable to: **The Lampo Group, Inc.**
                            783 Old Hickory Blvd, Suite 257 West
                            Brentwood, TN 37027

To phone in your order call: 615-371-8881 or 1-888-22PEACE

Product Description	Quantity	Price
_____	_____	$_____
_____	_____	$_____
TN residents add 8.25% sales tax		$_____
Shipping: Please add 5% ($5.00 min.)		$_____
Total Price		$_____

We Do Not accept CREDIT CARDS.
Orders are shipped the same day payment is received.

FOR THE BEST IN PAPERBACKS, LOOK FOR THE

In every corner of the world, on every subject under the sun, Penguin represents quality and variety—the very best in publishing today.

For complete information about books available from Penguin—including Penguin Classics, Penguin Compass, and Puffins—and how to order them, write to us at the appropriate address below. Please note that for copyright reasons the selection of books varies from country to country.

In the United States: Please write to *Penguin Group (USA), P.O. Box 12289 Dept. B, Newark, New Jersey 07101-5289* or call 1-800-788-6262.

In the United Kingdom: Please write to *Dept. EP, Penguin Books Ltd, Bath Road, Harmondsworth, West Drayton, Middlesex UB7 0DA*.

In Canada: Please write to *Penguin Books Canada Ltd, 90 Eglinton Avenue East, Suite 700, Toronto, Ontario M4P 2Y3*.

In Australia: Please write to *Penguin Books Australia Ltd, P.O. Box 257, Ringwood, Victoria 3134*.

In New Zealand: Please write to *Penguin Books (NZ) Ltd, Private Bag 102902, North Shore Mail Centre, Auckland 10*.

In India: Please write to *Penguin Books India Pvt Ltd, 11 Panchsheel Shopping Centre, Panchsheel Park, New Delhi 110 017*.

In the Netherlands: Please write to *Penguin Books Netherlands bv, Postbus 3507, NL-1001 AH Amsterdam*.

In Germany: Please write to *Penguin Books Deutschland GmbH, Metzlerstrasse 26, 60594 Frankfurt am Main*.

In Spain: Please write to *Penguin Books S. A., Bravo Murillo 19, 1° B, 28015 Madrid*.

In Italy: Please write to *Penguin Italia s.r.l., Via Benedetto Croce 2, 20094 Corsico, Milano*.

In France: Please write to *Penguin France, Le Carré Wilson, 62 rue Benjamin Baillaud, 31500 Toulouse*.

In Japan: Please write to *Penguin Books Japan Ltd, Kaneko Building, 2-3-25 Koraku, Bunkyo-Ku, Tokyo 112*.

In South Africa: Please write to *Penguin Books South Africa (Pty) Ltd, Private Bag X14, Parkview, 2122 Johannesburg*.